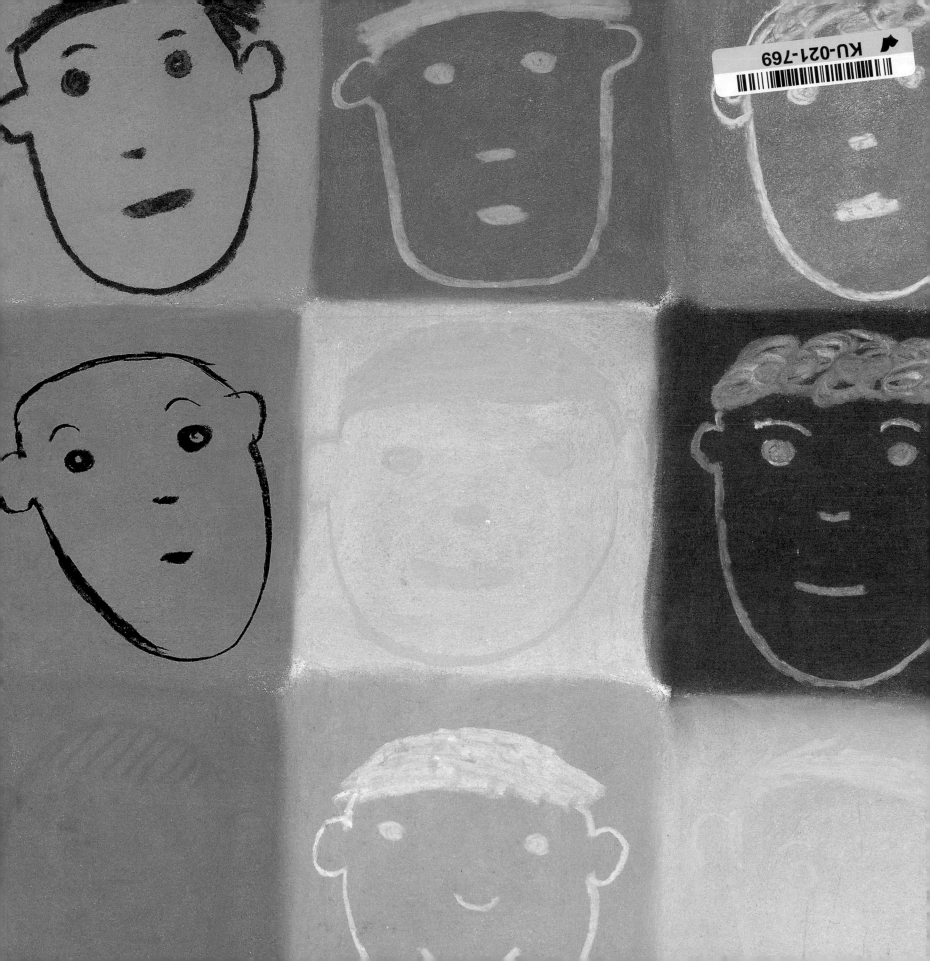

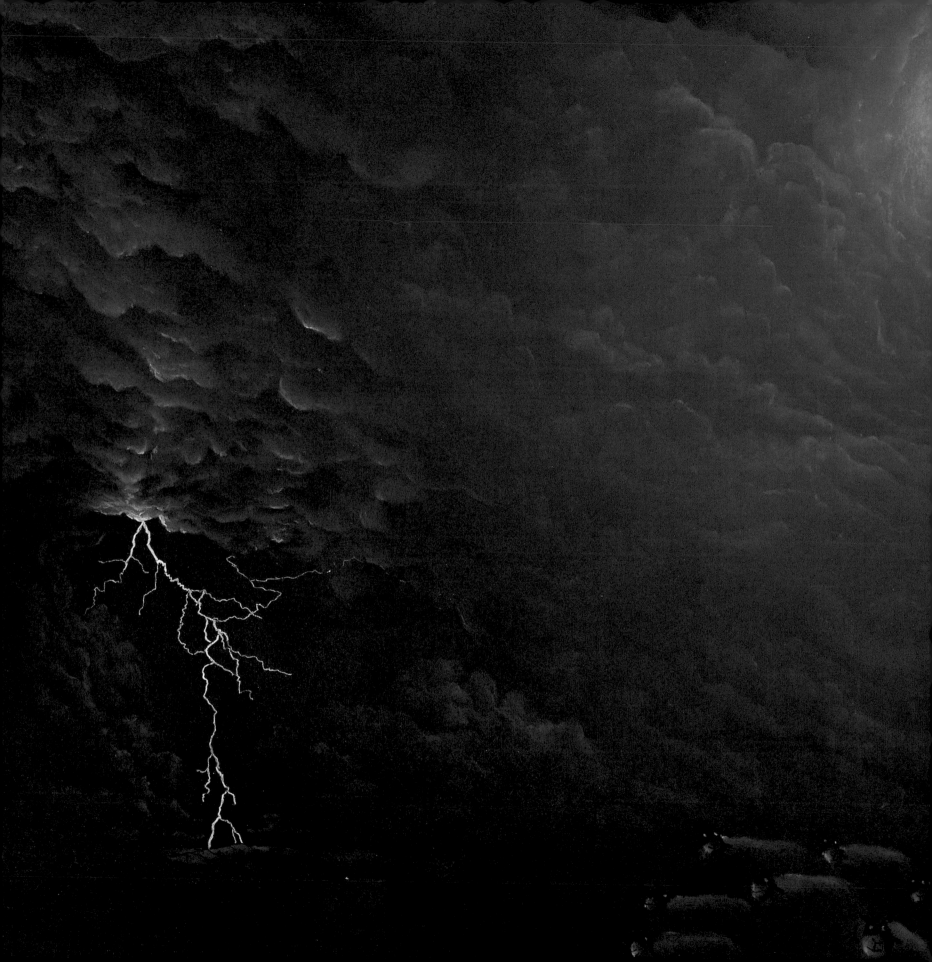

MACKENZIE THORPE

FROM THE HEART

A Byron Preiss Book

UNIVERSE

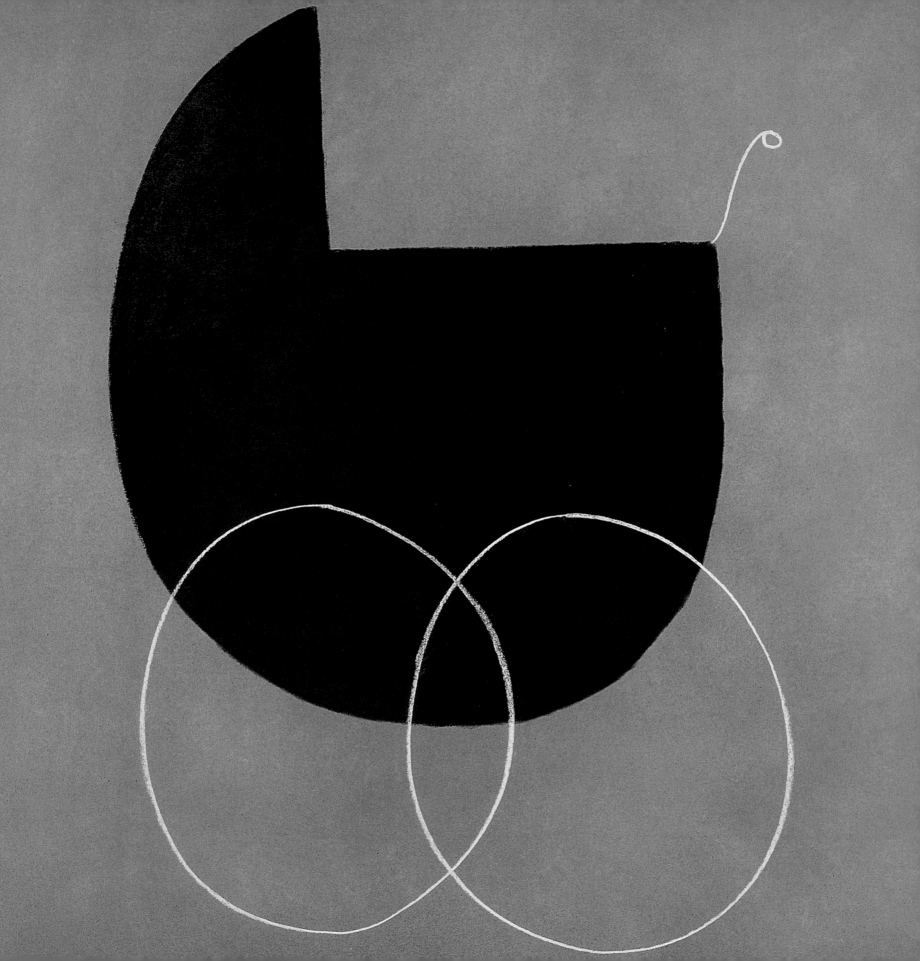

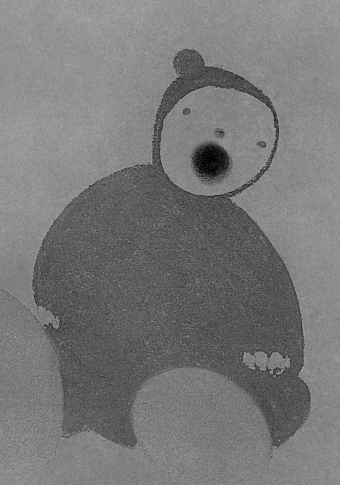

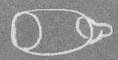

Cover picture: The Last Temptation
Front endpaper: Boys' Heads–Class
Back endpaper: Girls' Heads–Class
Half-title: The Drip
Title: Forward
Contents: Cuckoo in the Nest
This page: The Horizon

First published in the United States of America in 2000
by UNIVERSE PUBLISHING
A division of Rizzoli International Publications, Inc.
300 Park Avenue South
New York, NY 10010

Copyright © by Mackenzie Thorpe and Byron Preiss Visual
Publications, Inc.

00 01 02 03/10 9 8 7 6 5 4 3 2

Designed by Guy Callaby and Michael Haines
for Threefold Limited, London

Edited by Dinah Dunn

Printed in England

Library of Congress Cataloging-in-Publication Data is available
upon request

This book is about the truth,
a truth for so many.
A truth that shows the color
and hope within life's struggles.

Mackenzie Thorpe 2000

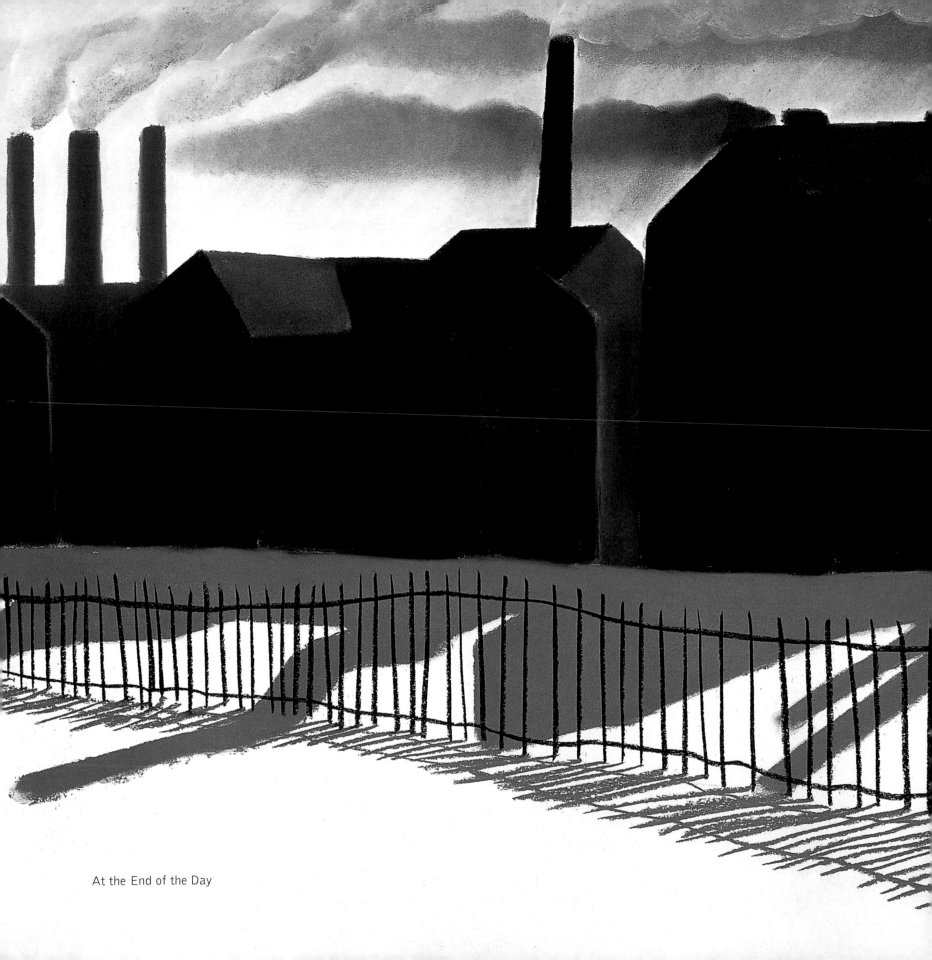

At the End of the Day

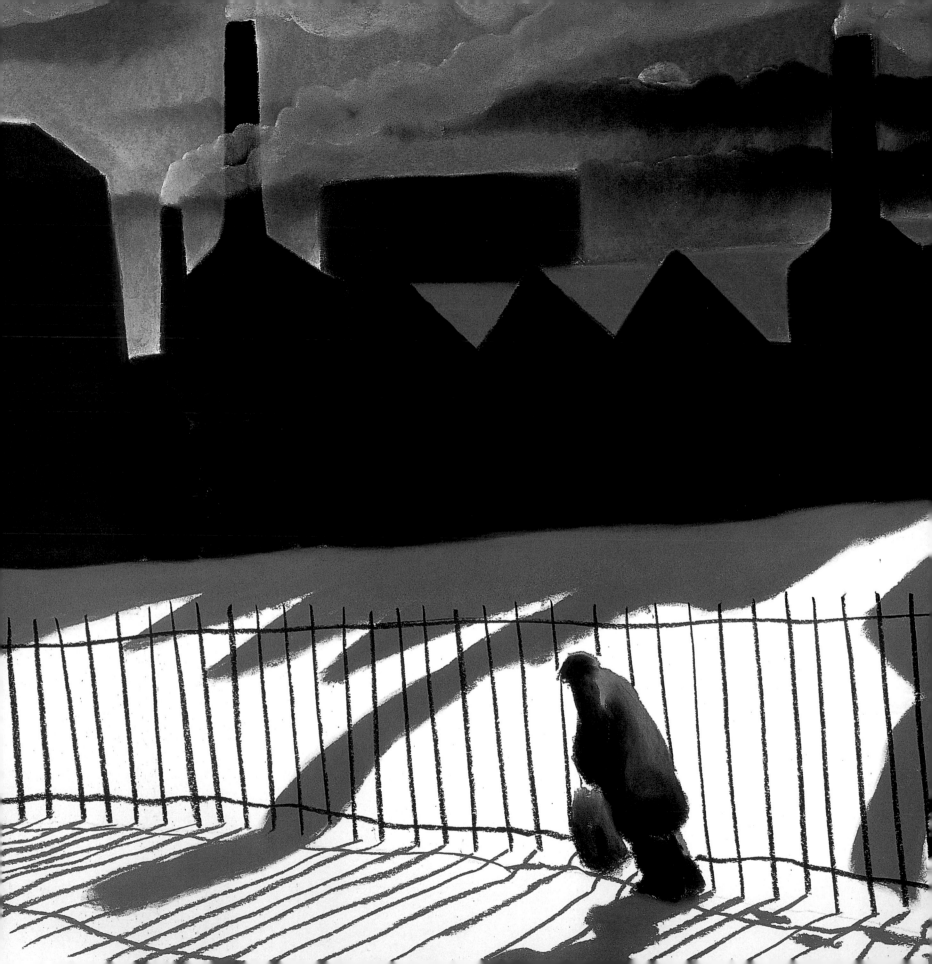

When I first set up the Art Haus shop in North Yorkshire, money didn't come easily. My work was still developing and was not widely understood. That's when I did the first square sheep. I didn't think about what I was doing when I painted it. I just drew this shape and then put a head and legs on it and it became my self-portrait, standing solid, facing the world for all to see.

I had studied art therapy, so I knew that the canvas, no matter what its size, is the universe and whatever art is placed on it is within that universe. If you look at my world on the canvas, you've got this big square shape and it's a self-portrait. So I was filling that universe with me, standing tall, with four legs on the ground, the landscape behind me, and my head touching the sky.

I understood later why the sheep was square. It represented society's narrow-mindedness and rejection of things new or different. But after I had a near-fatal car accident, the sheep came to mean something different to me, more to do with my wife and kids. My family is one of the biggest influences on me now, I love them with all of my heart. I'll draw a picture and it'll be so bright, I'll like it so much that I'll call it "Owen" or "Chloe" or "Susan," because I want them to have it, it's for them. It's about the love and closeness we are so privileged to share.

Painting the square sheep was a way of empowering myself, like putting feelings down on paper so they could reflect back to me. You would think that when I'm working on pictures of big smiley faces, I must be really happy. Sometimes it's the other way around. It allows me to move on in times of depression or anger. When I work in that way my mood lifts and I start having a ball—putting the piece of paper up, turning on some loud, inspiring music, then drawing a big smiley face. I change the focus of my mood. I wasn't aware of it until my wife Susan pointed it out. It's a way of saying you can be happy if you choose to be.

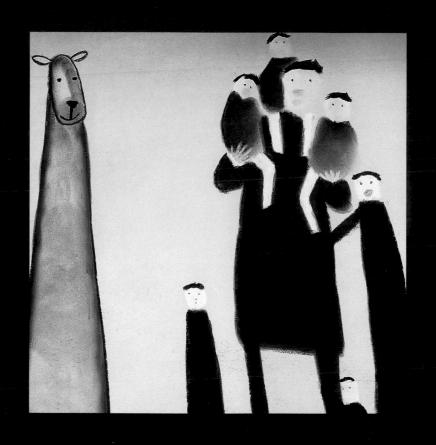

Love and Family

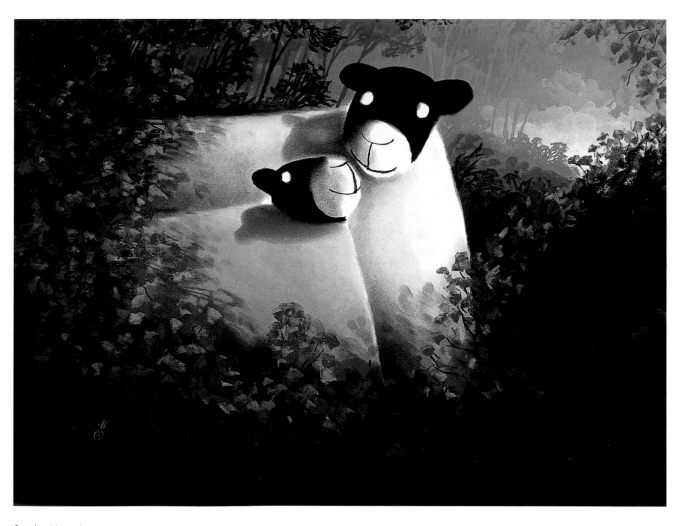

In the Woods

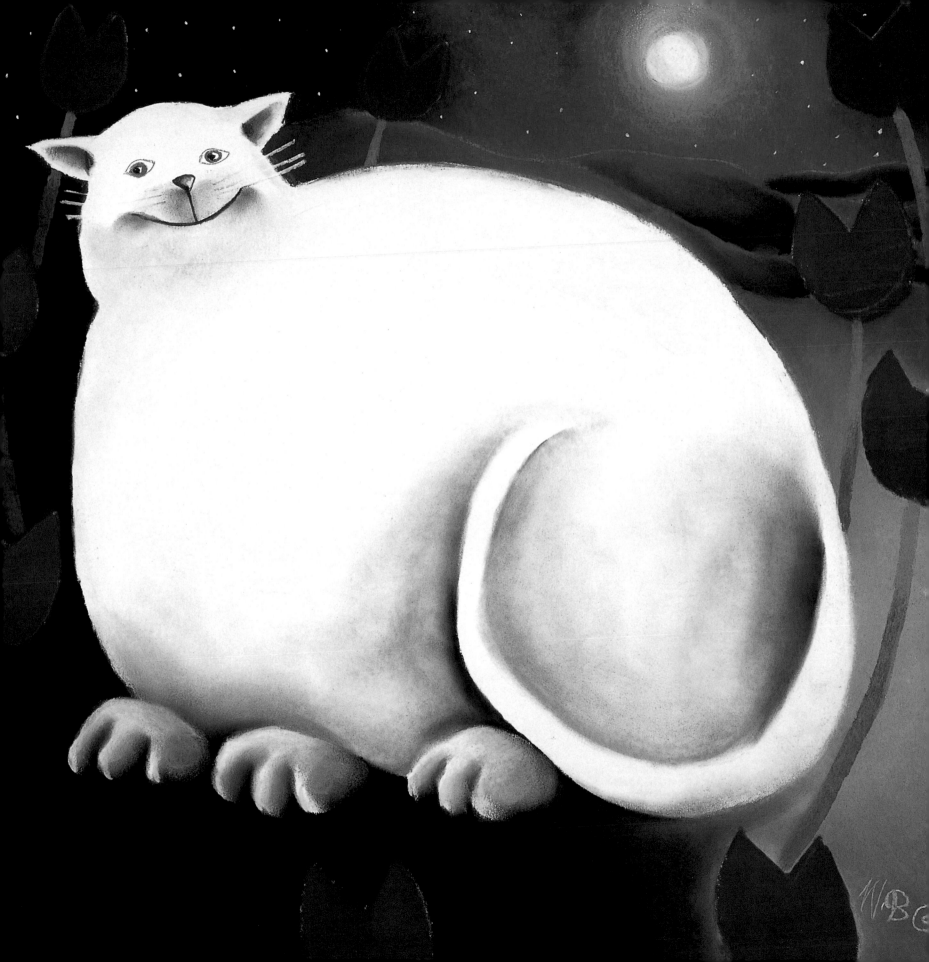

ANIMALS I don't see the point in painting a portrait—you might as well take a photograph. But to paint someone's personality, what's beneath the surface, is much more meaningful. So, I'll paint someone as a big smiley giraffe or a horse with its mane blowing in the wind to show the different sides of their personality.

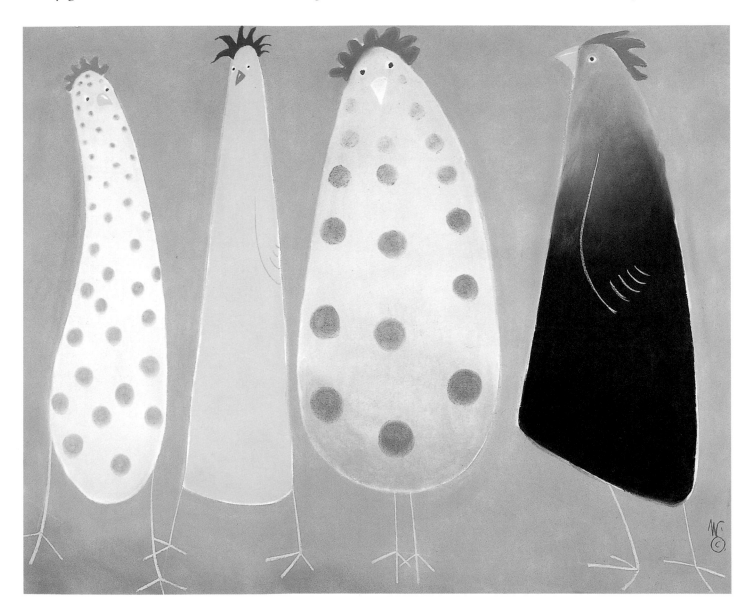

Cock-a-Doodle-Doo

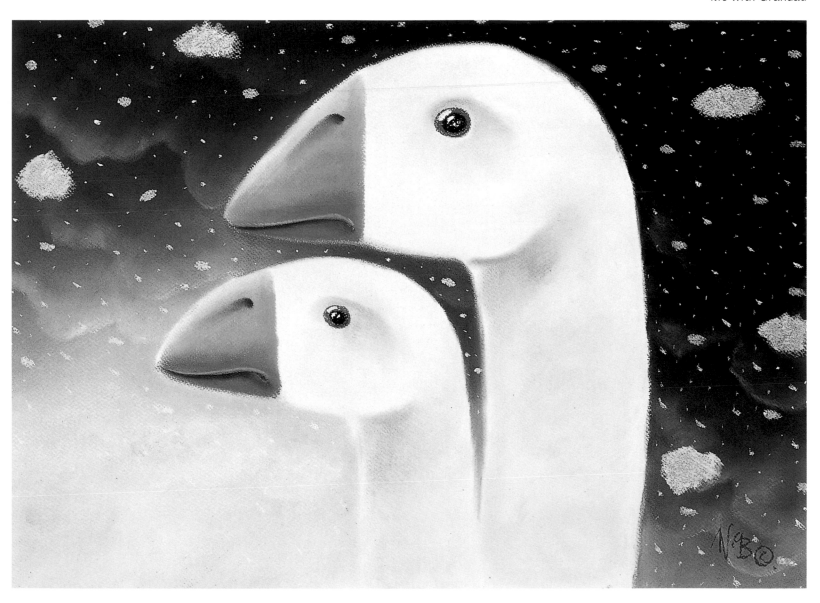

Overleaf
Love His Mane   Lawrence II   Endless Love

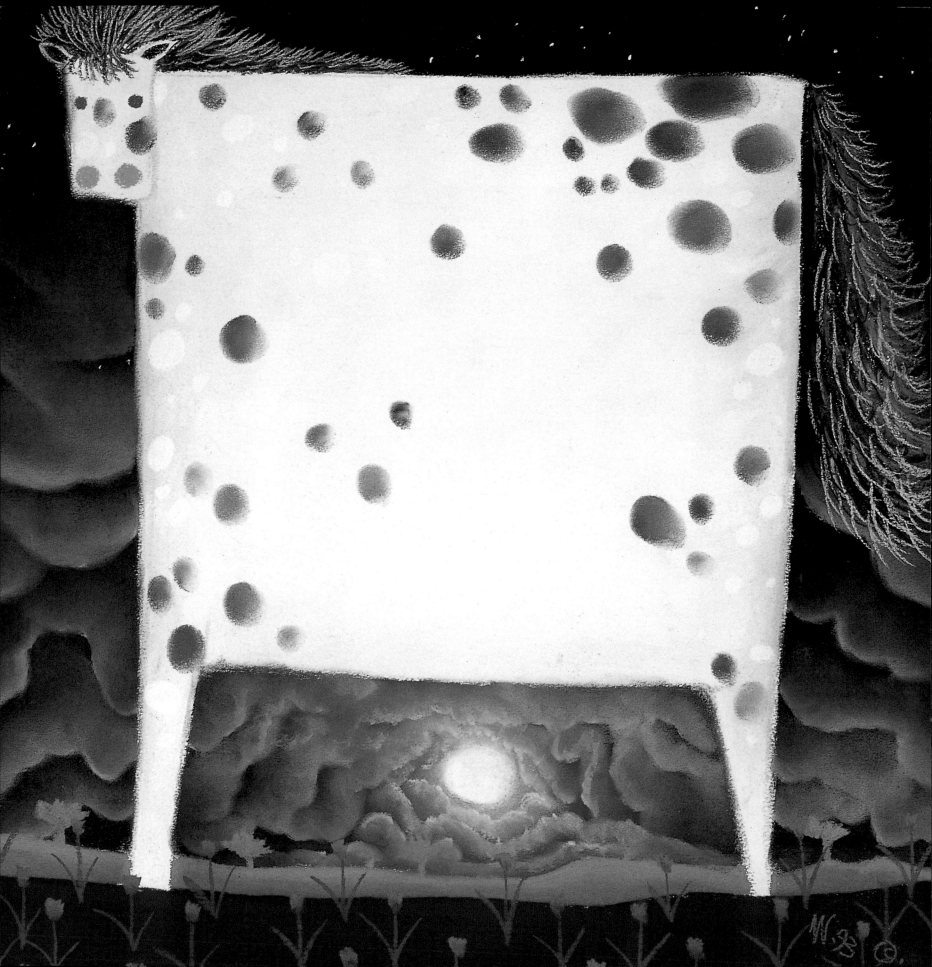

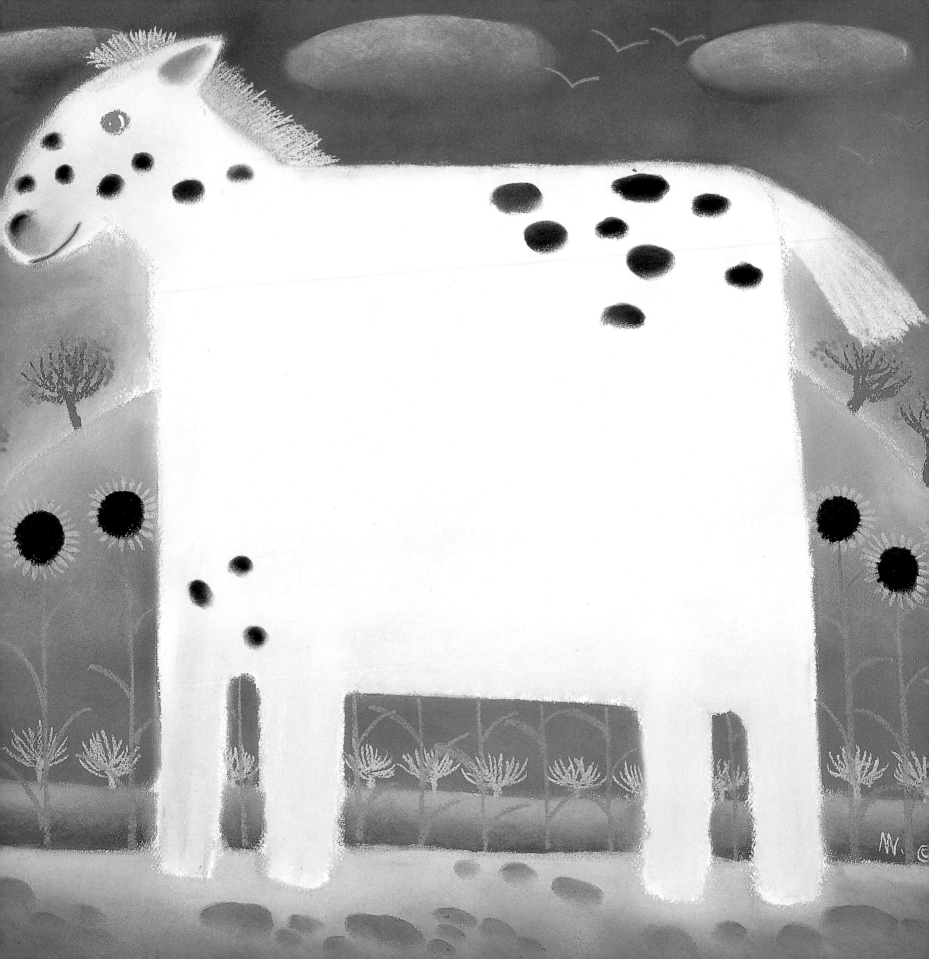

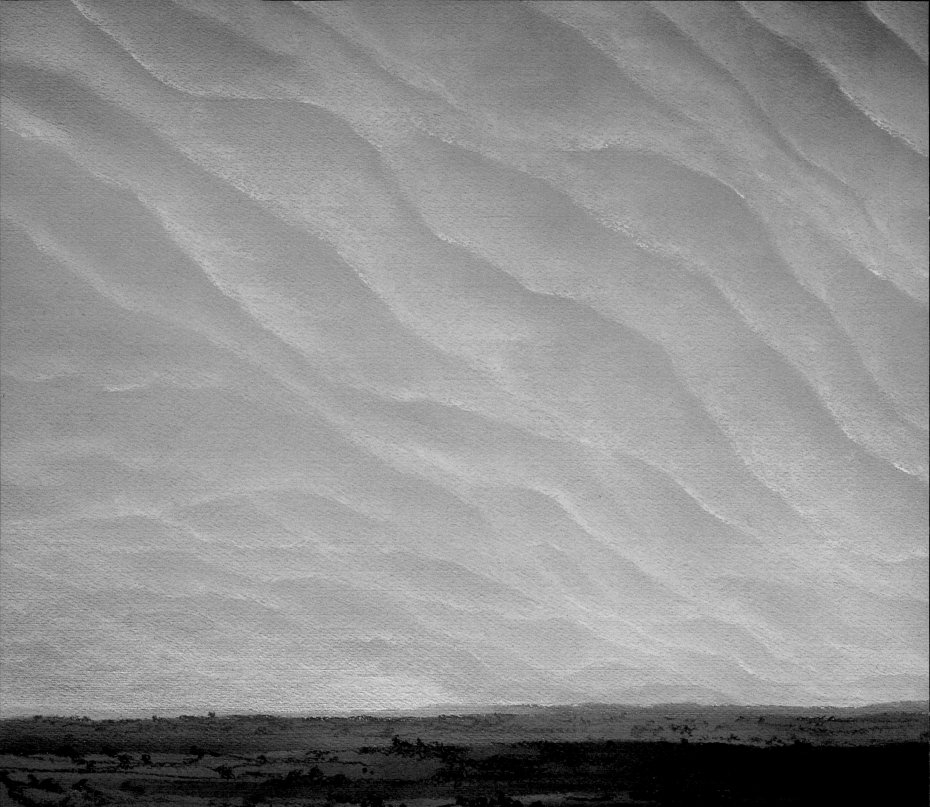

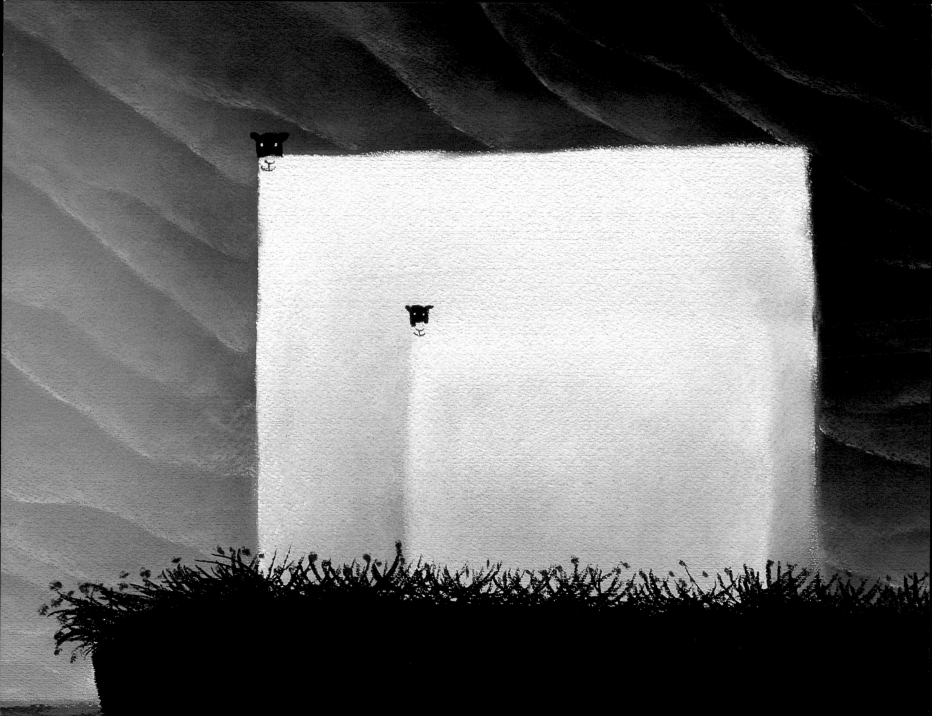

A Bleating Heart

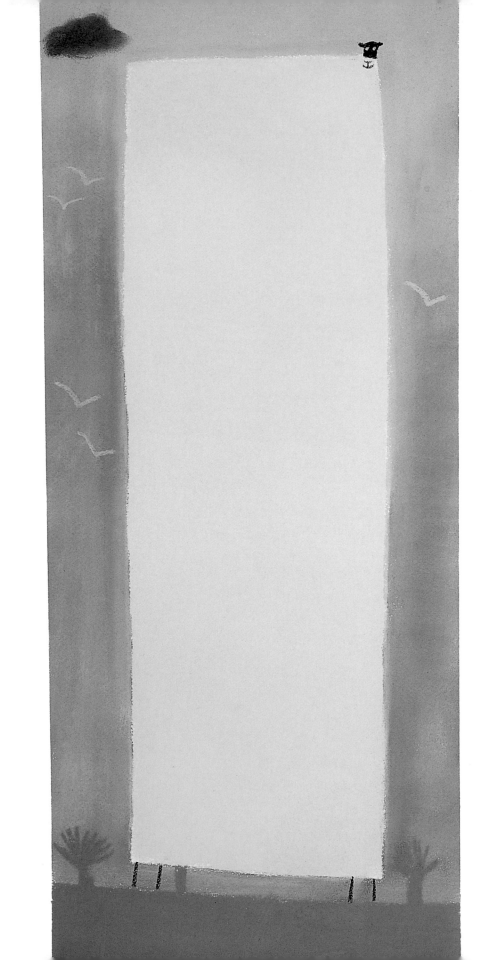

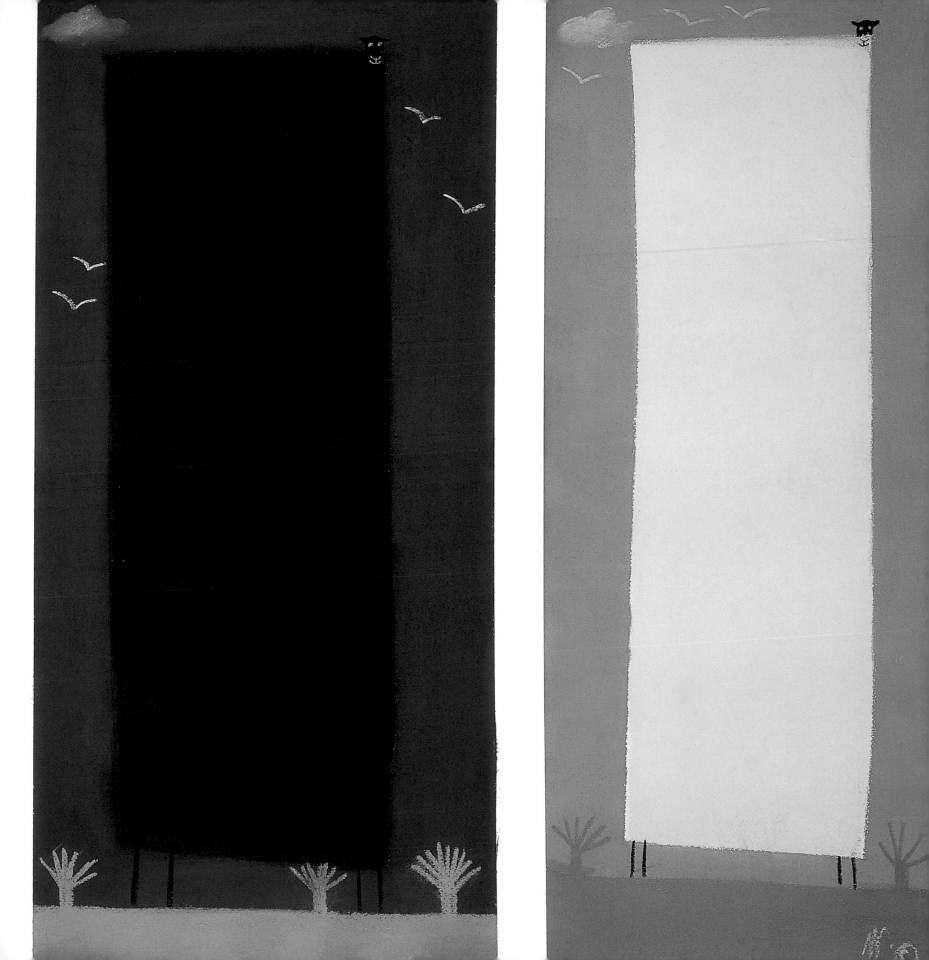

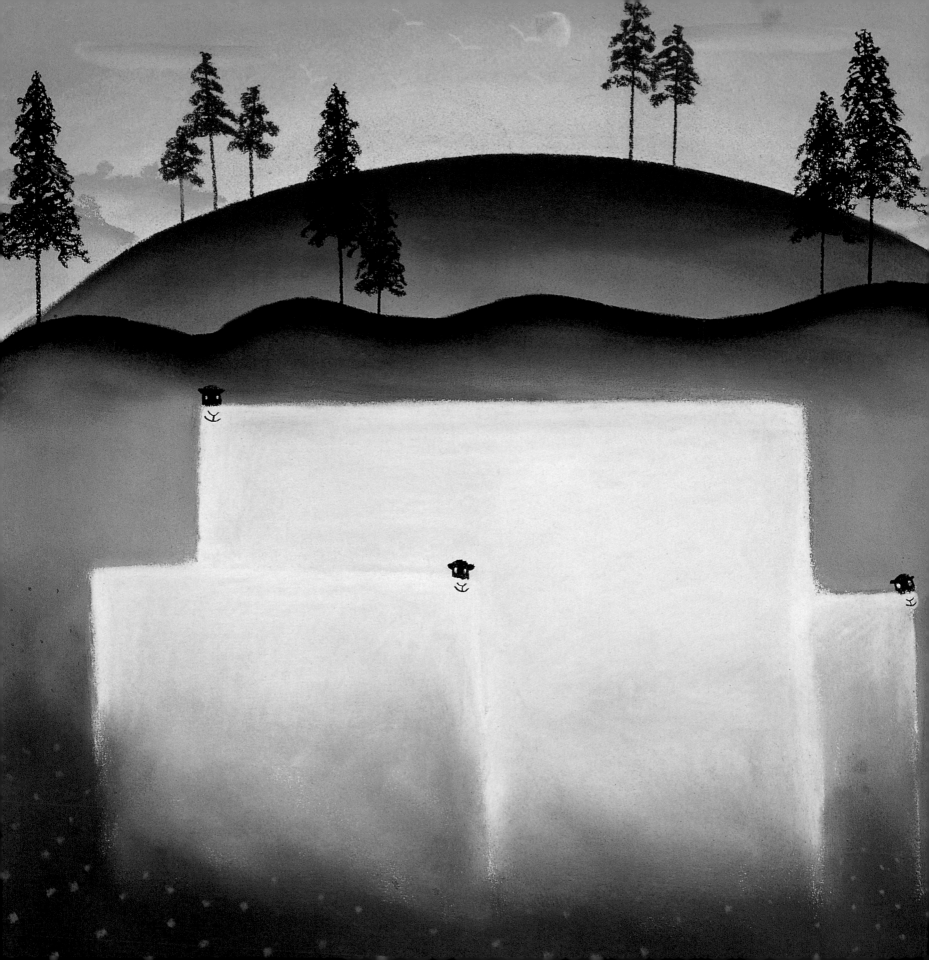

The Family

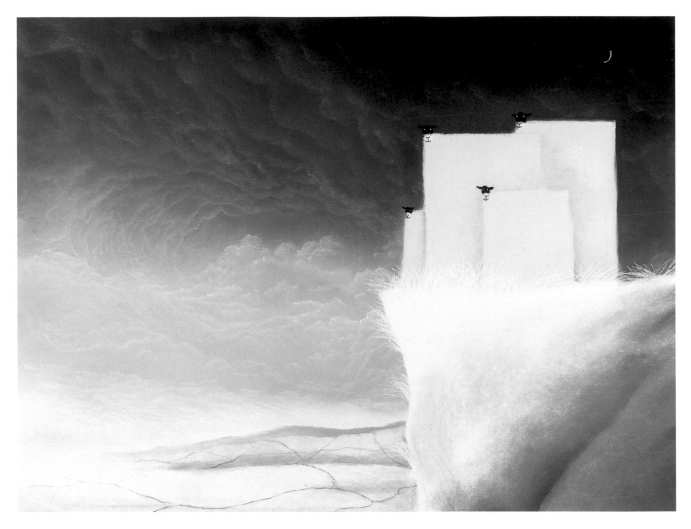

In the Heart of Winter

SUNFLOWERS

Sunflowers are a tribute to Van Gogh. When I first saw *Lust for Life*, the film about Van Gogh's life and work, I realized that I had the same drive to paint, no matter what the odds. I understood that I wasn't here to work in the shipyards, but that my purpose was to paint the truth in my life.

The Sunshine of My Life

From the **moon**
The **eyes**
Of her **soul**
From the **hands**
Through my **heart**

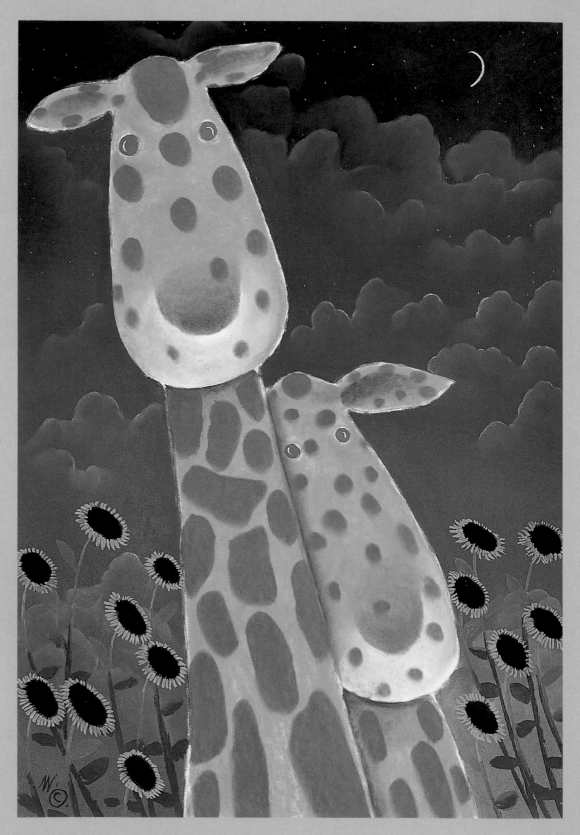

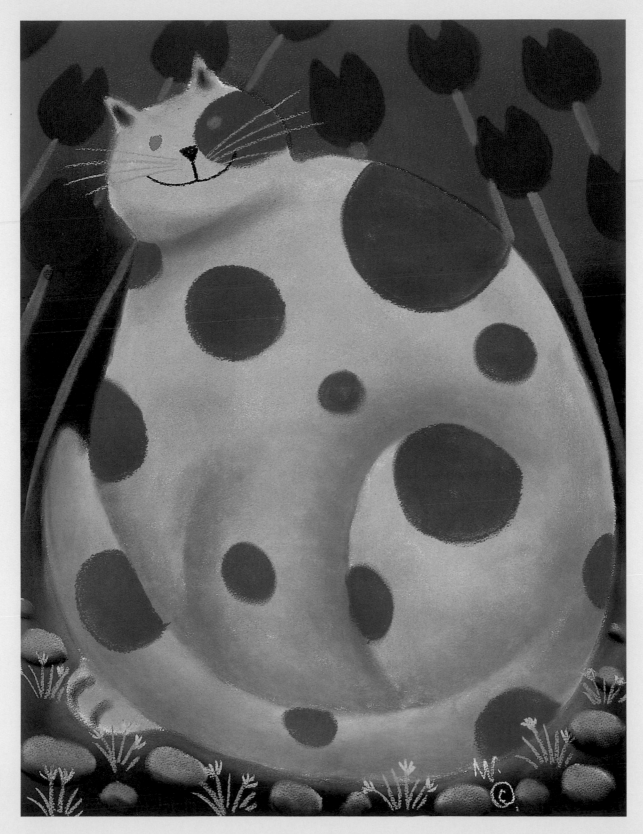

Susan

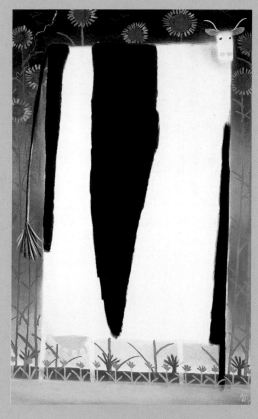

Susan

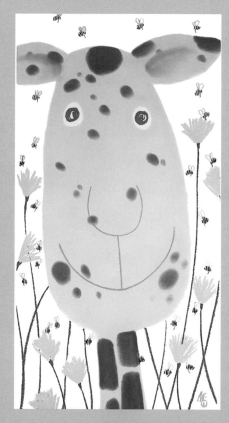

Chloe

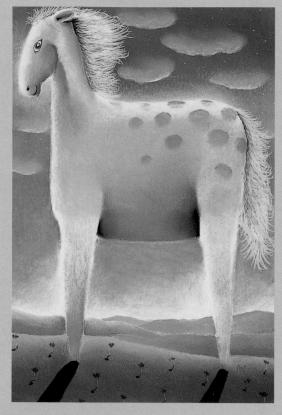

Owen

OWEN AND CHLOE Sometimes I wake up in the morning and feel a bit down. I will go into the kitchen and Chloe will be there, my lovely fourteen year old, talking and laughing, gossiping like all teenage girls do, moaning about her hair or school or whatever. I can always get a hug from her and feel so privileged. Owen is sixteen, taller than me now. I'm so proud of him. He is so much fun. He doesn't fight or steal or get into trouble—he's just a nice guy. Whenever I feel the slightest bit down, I only have to think about these two, look out of the window and think how good it all is.

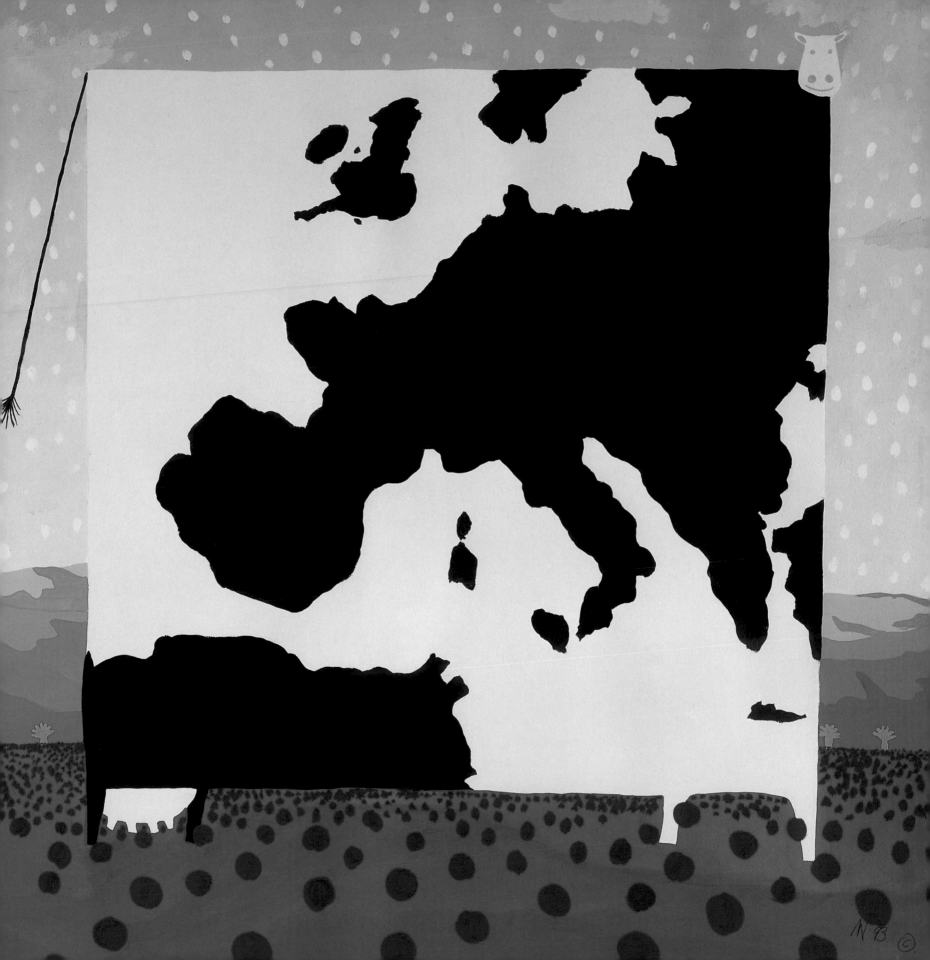

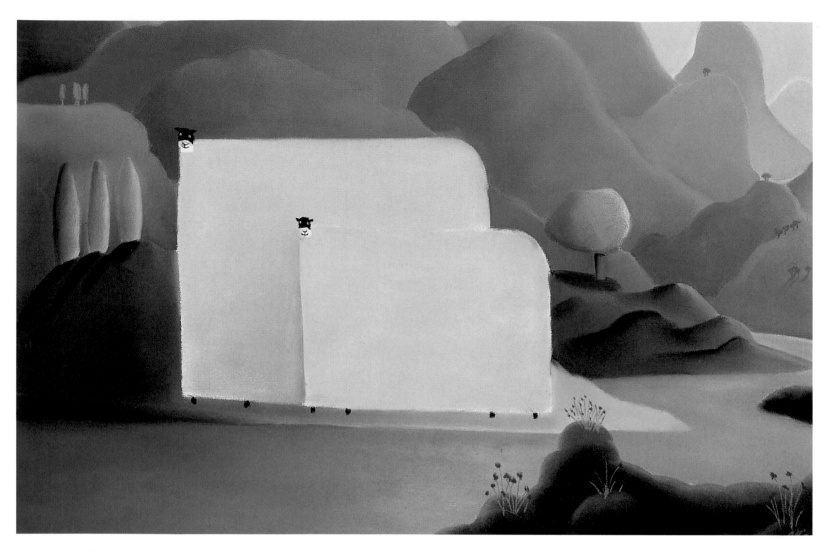

In the Land of Love

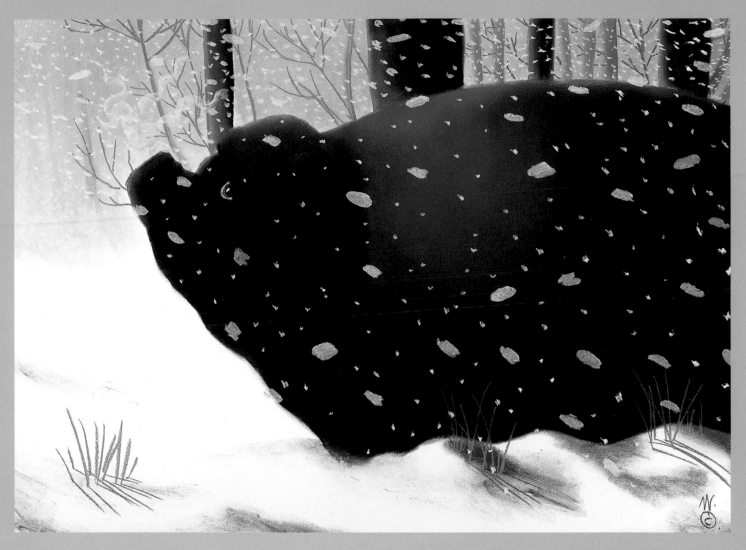

Pig in Snow

Taking the Dog Out

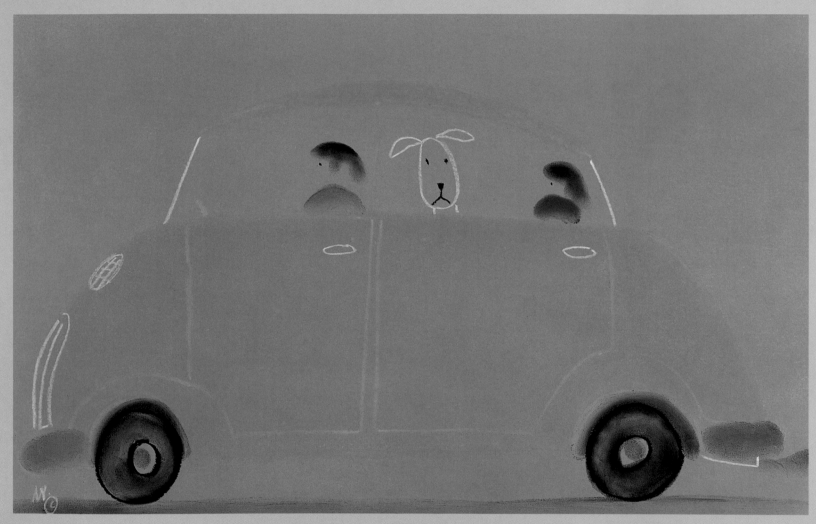

Front and Side Elevation

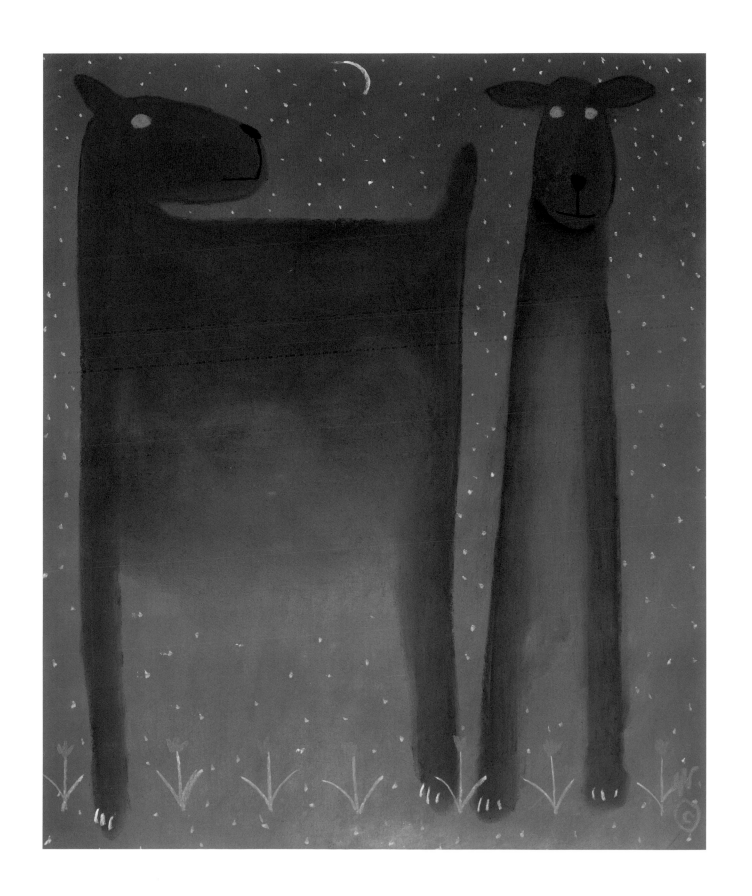

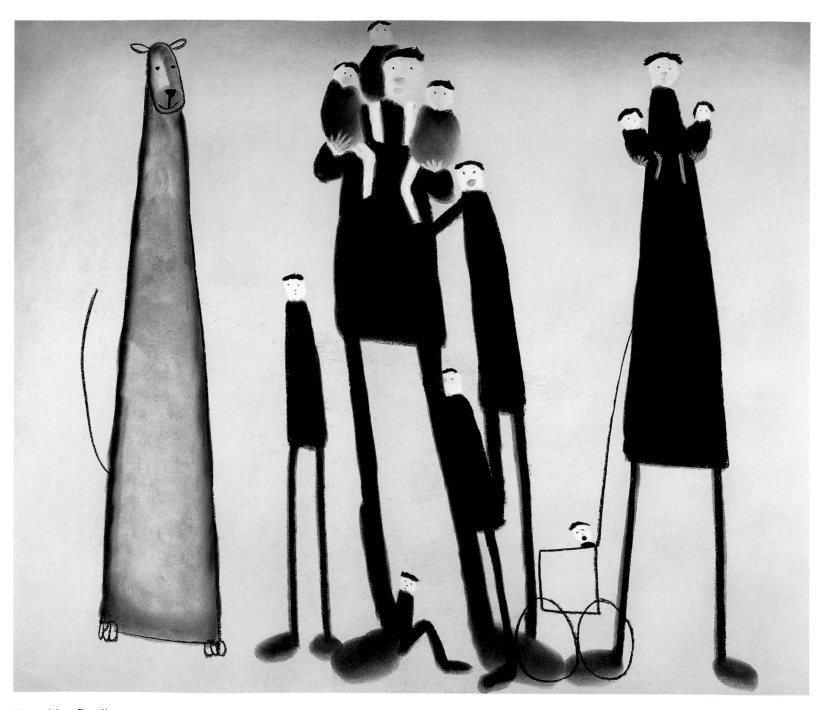

Dog with a Family

Leading the Bull

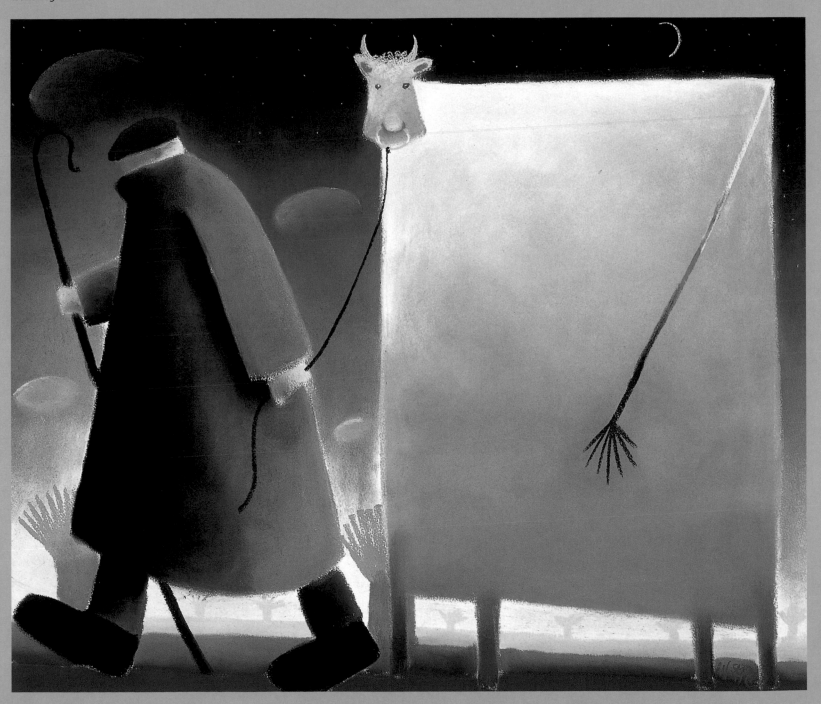

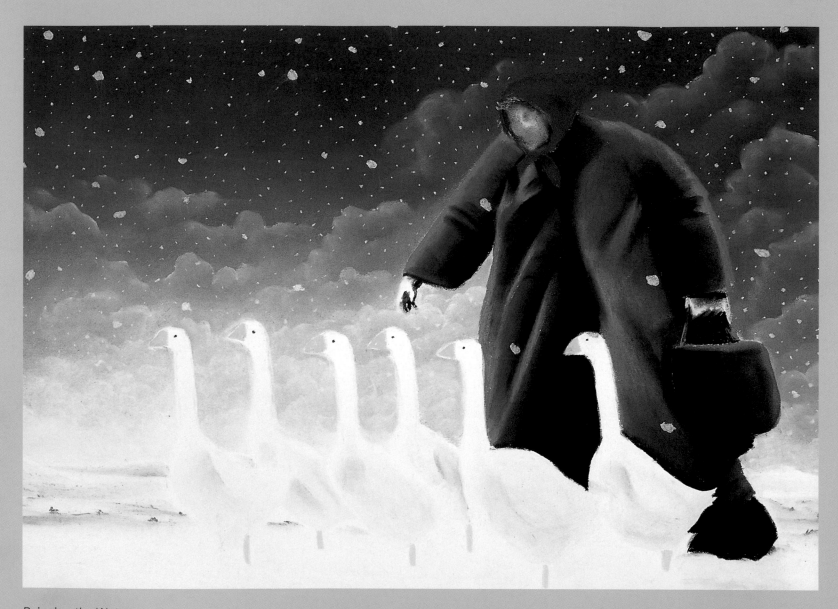

Bringing the Water

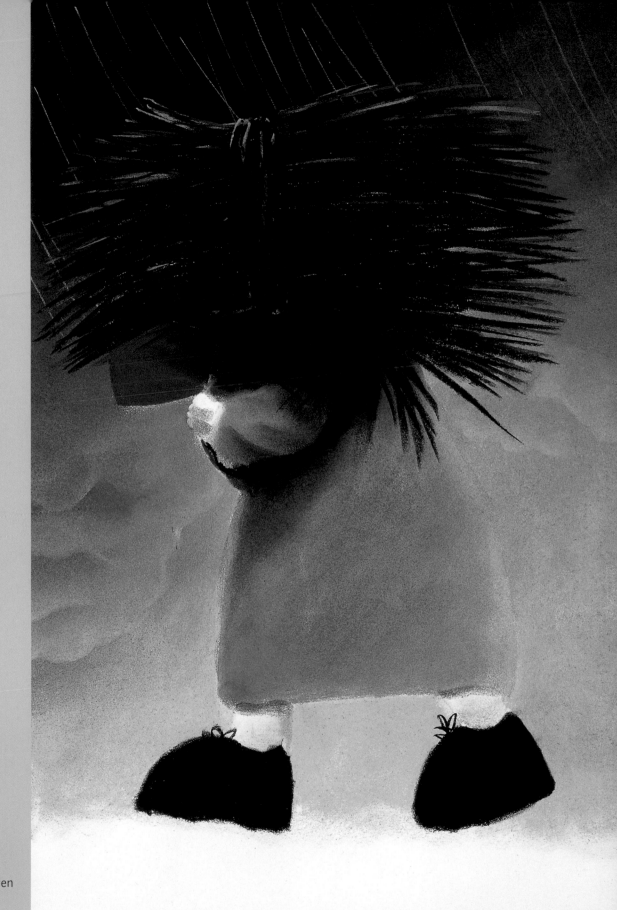

Underburden

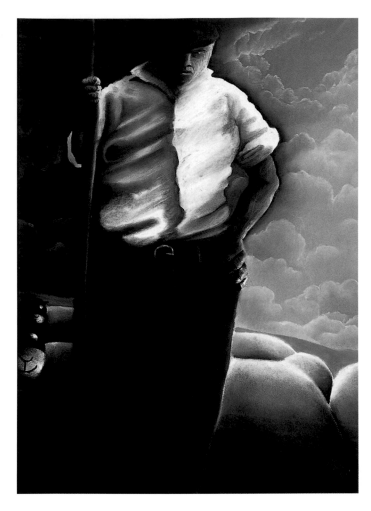

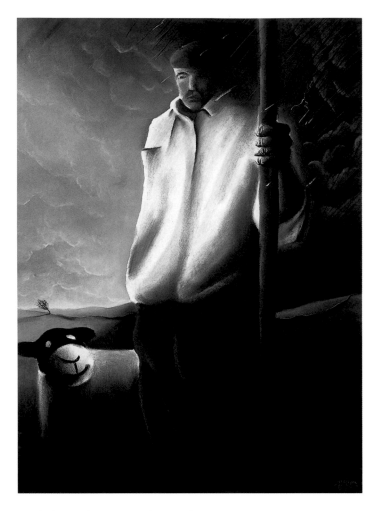

Before the Wind Blows

A Little Further Down the Road

SHEPHERDS I'm a man who is able to wash his own clothes. I do ironing, I cook and clean and I go to work. I don't have any problems with this. I do these things because I want clean clothes and we need to eat and these are not difficult tasks. I expect to share the workload, I want to be a good and fair person, and I don't have to live by other people's rules of what a man should and should not do.

The shepherd in my work is that all-around person—not just a man, but a person. This shepherd will walk through the wilderness; he will stand atop the highest mountains; he will go without food and shelter to look after his flock. I want to be a man who will look after a child, care for his flock, protect them, love, guide, and nurture them. I will do whatever it takes to keep them safe and happy.

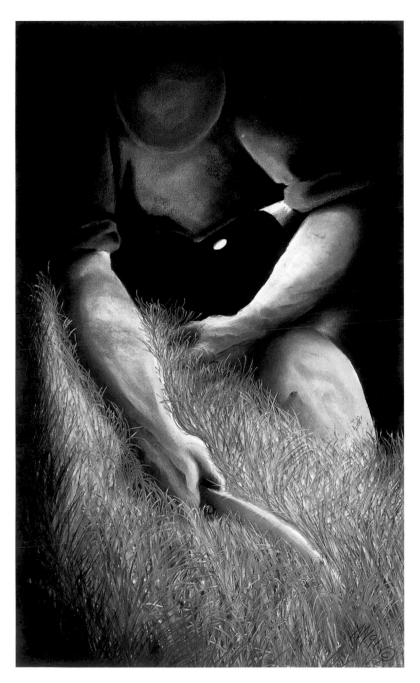

I Saw the Light

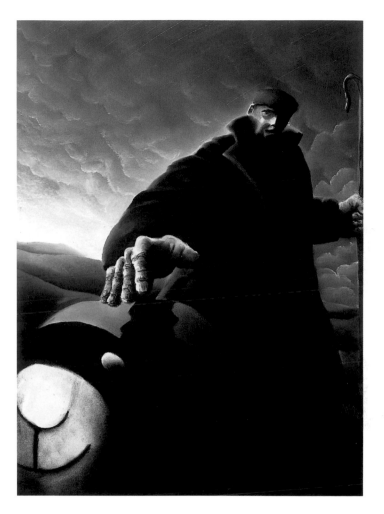

Reach Out and Touch

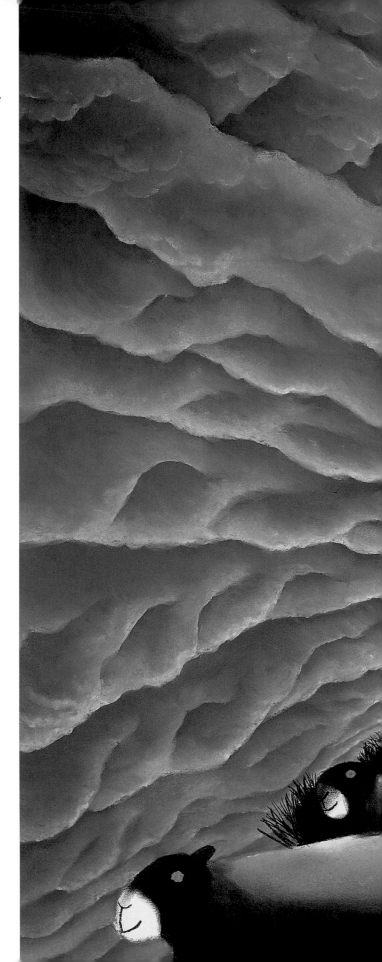

With all my heart and passion...

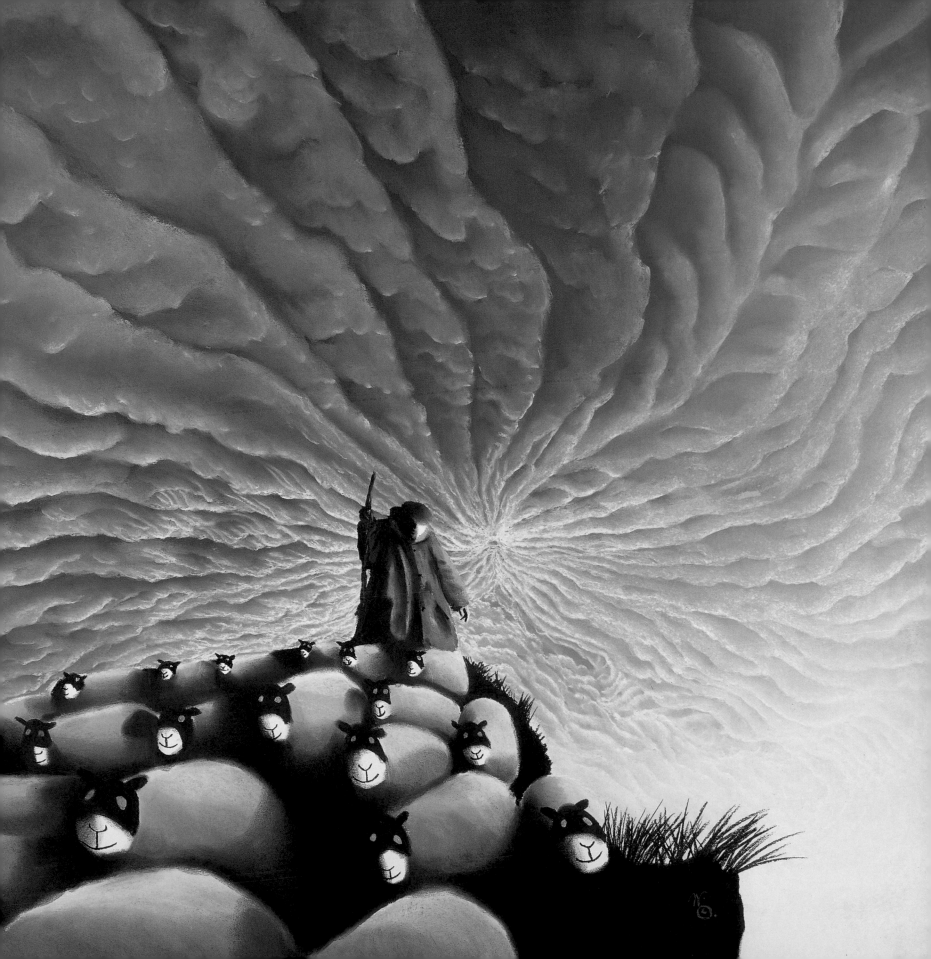

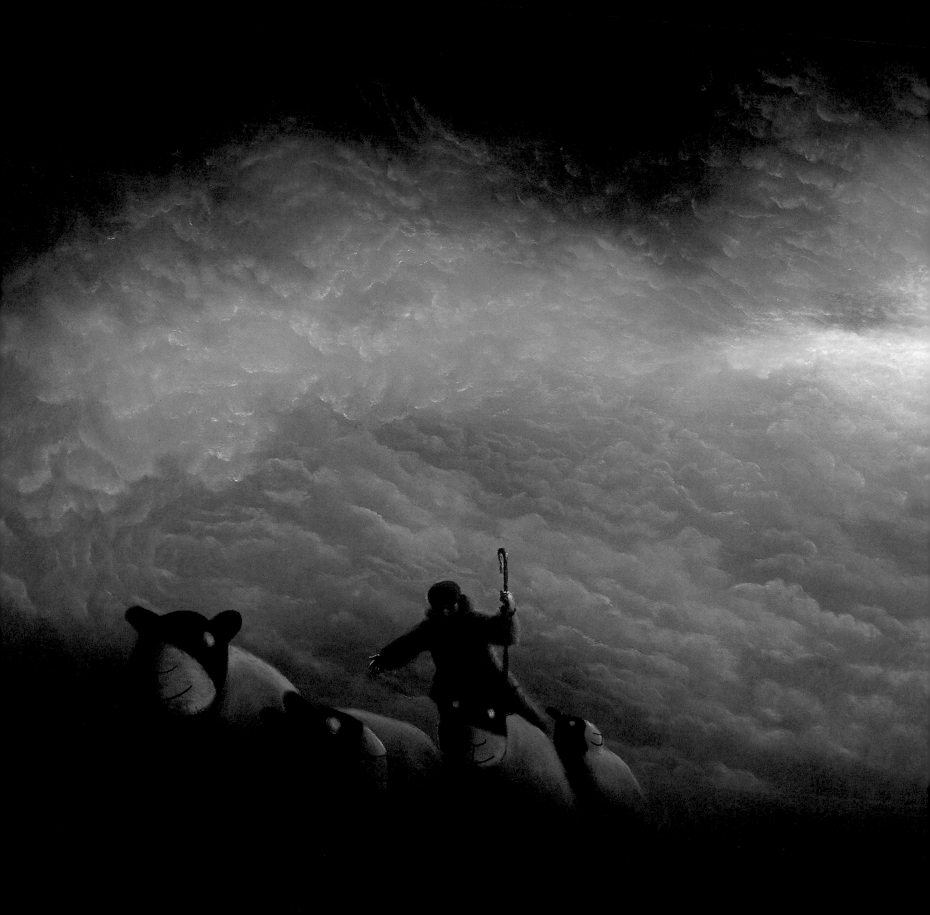

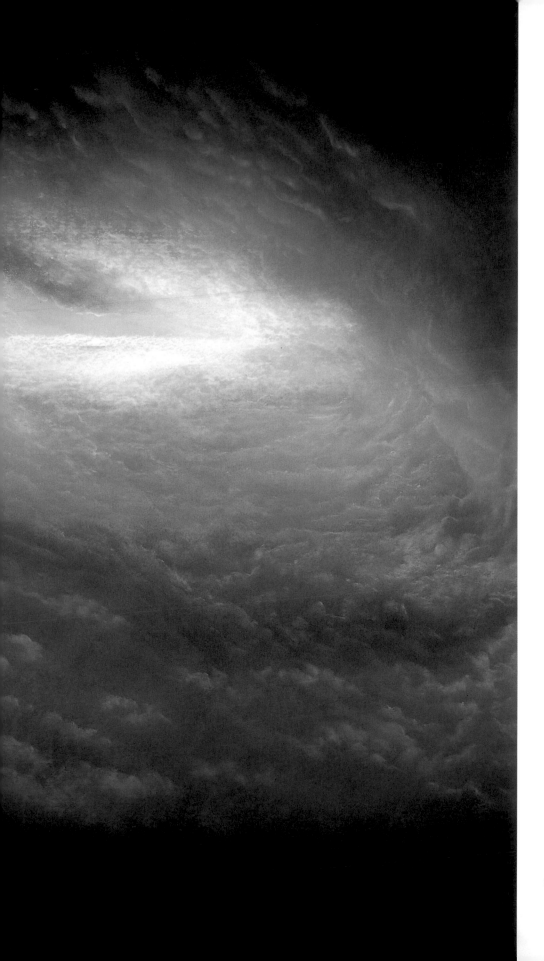

...no

matter

what,

we

will

come

through.

Getting There

I was born in my grandmother's living room in the heart of Middlesbrough, by the majestic transporter bridge. Eleven of us lived there, all crowded together. Inside of that house I was safe, eating grandma's apple pie, sitting on grandad's knee. Outside I was vulnerable. I didn't fit in either at school or on the street. Reading and writing seemed impossible for me to master. I was not a good fighter, nor a streetwise little toughie. My uncle Lawrence, who was three years older, protected me. He held himself well in that environment, he spoke the right language, the language of the streets. I could only draw and that set me apart even further. I got picked on, I got shouted at, I got humiliated, I got knocked down. I guess I retreated into myself as a means of protection, to stop the rejection and isolation I felt from hurting too much.

It was twenty years before my wife, Susan, came into my life and for the first time I felt it was safe to show my love, passion, and joy, freely and openly. A lot of my paintings of children are saying, "Just give me a chance. Don't step over me, don't disregard me, don't hurt me. Love and respect me."

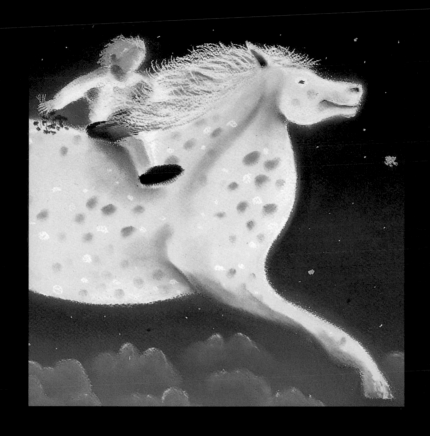

When We Were Young

Flower Girl

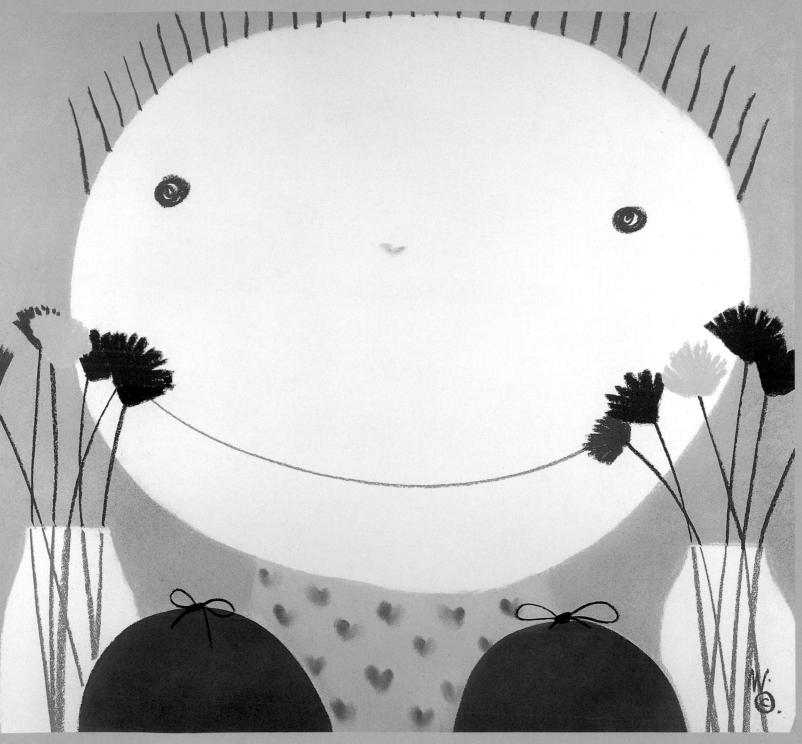

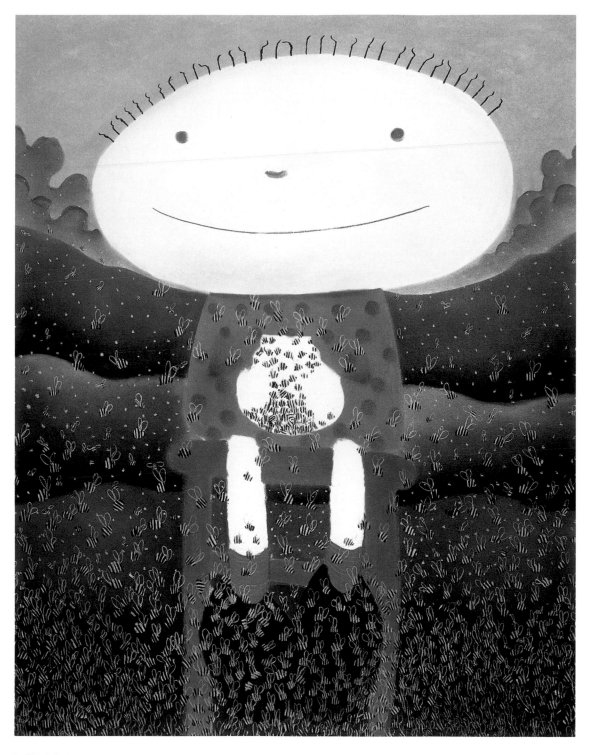

BEES The first time I drew a bee, I wanted to put a little "bzzzz" into the picture because sound is a part of life. I started to employ it more and more. But then I got stung on the arm by a bee and it swelled so big I couldn't bend it. If I had been in the wilderness and was stung on my throat or my head, would I have died, my airways swollen, gasping for breath? This tiny little bee could have been my downfall. I feel it was a reminder not to overlook things in life.

Self with Bees

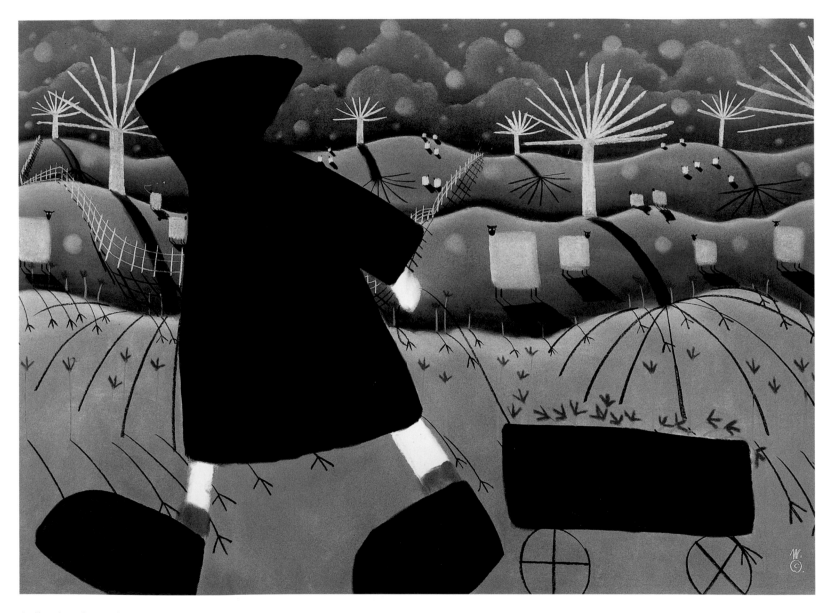

Collecting the Red

CHILDREN WITH FLOWERS Children are
the source of love—they plant it at our feet,
nurture it, and help it grow throughout our lives.

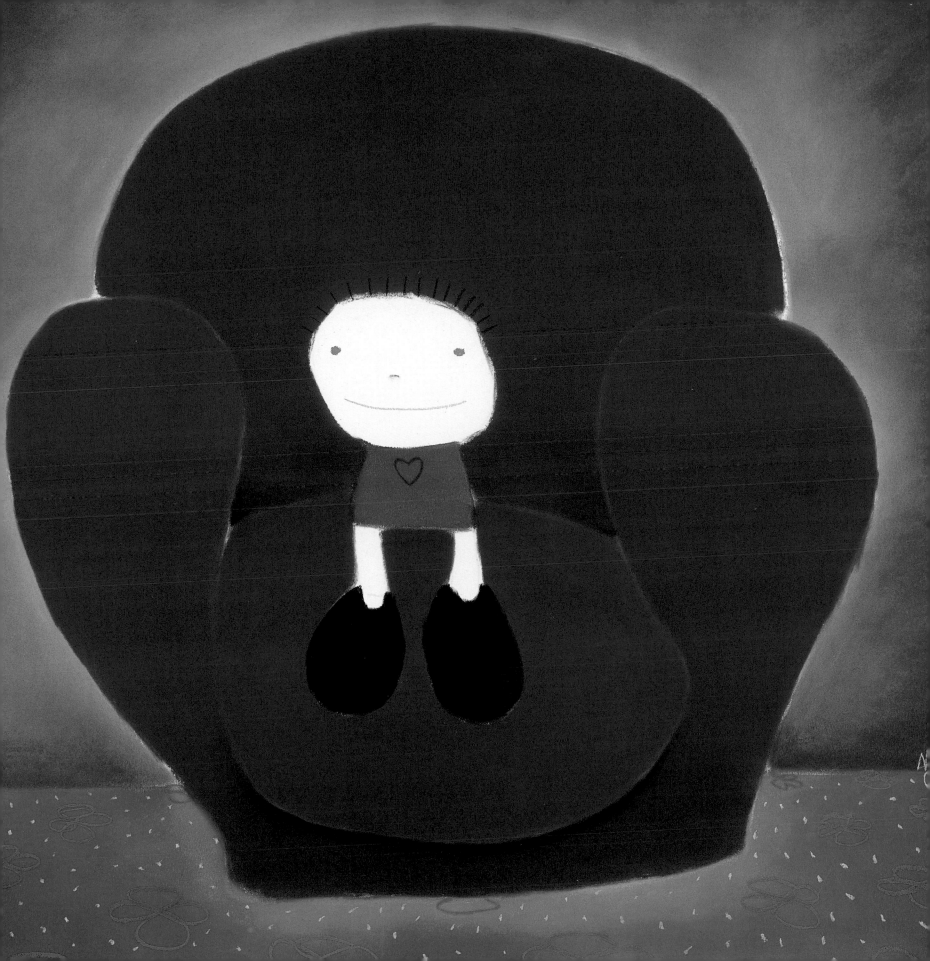

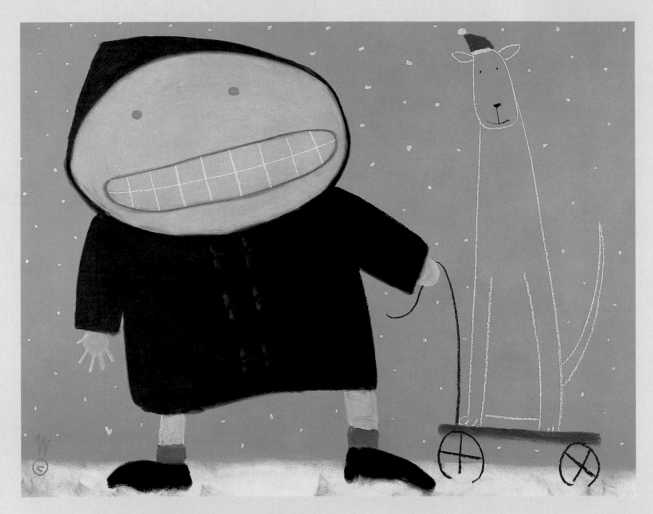

Avalon

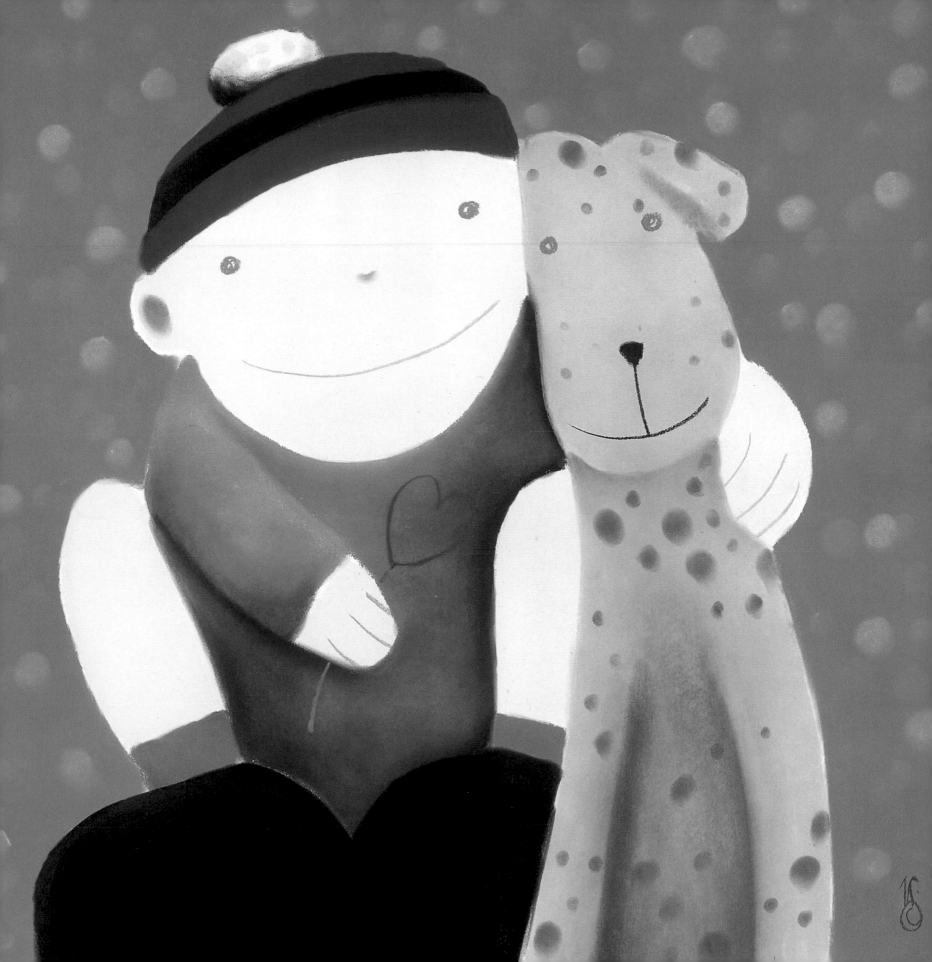

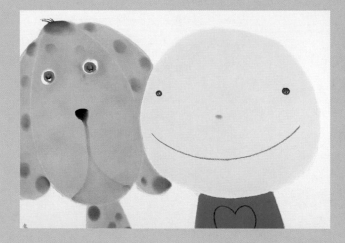

Love and Joy

BIG HEADS The idea is that we are all born the same, equal. As we grow, we impose restrictions on ourselves and on our children. We are not born afraid of the dark. We are not born racists. We are not born frightened of spiders. We learn to be scared of new adventures, of new foods, of new experiences, and so our world shrinks. This fear is all between our ears—it's not real. Yet we persist in living it and passing it on instead of welcoming and sharing the joy of the new and the unknown. For me, the big heads symbolize children: new, uncorrupted, their heads full of endless possibility, open to whatever comes their way. It is only as we grow older that we become narrow and closed. Let's keep our heads as big as possible. Continue to marvel at the beauty of nature, revel in the smell of the flowers, and thank God you're alive.

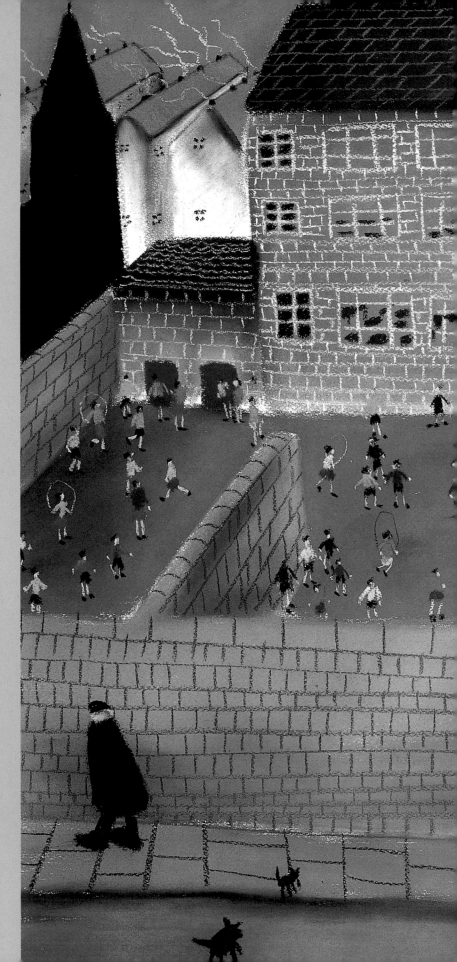

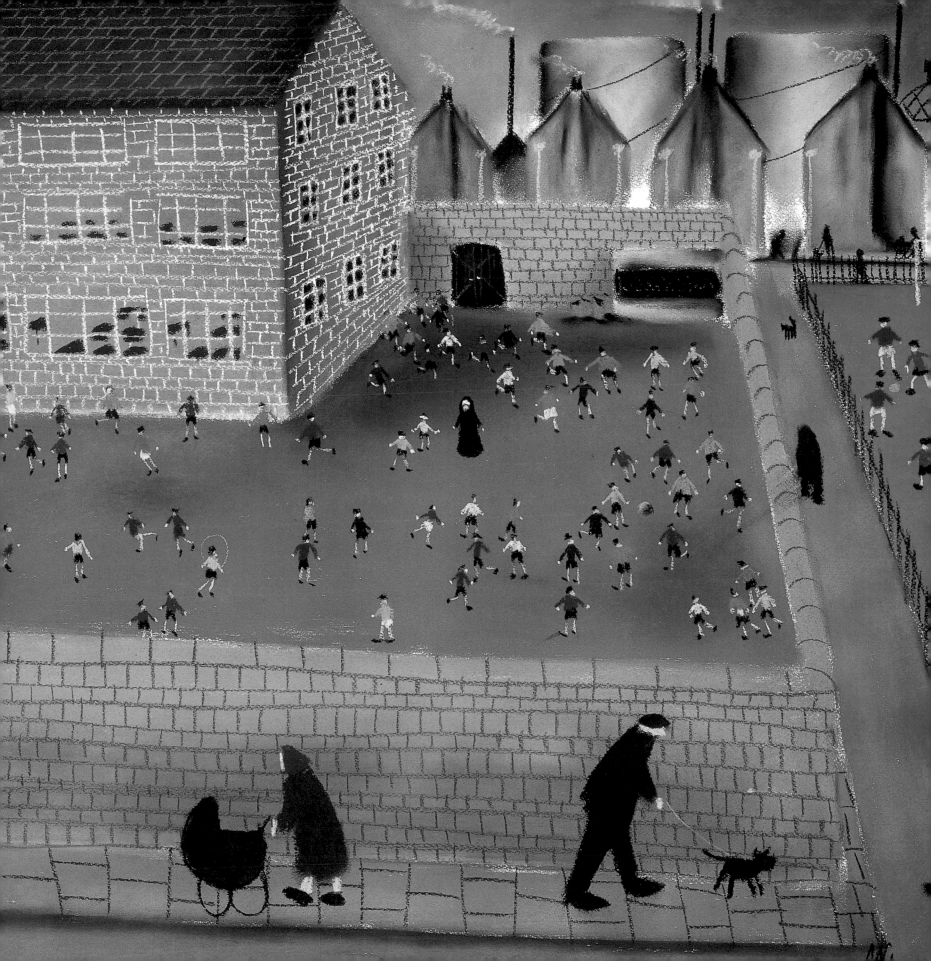

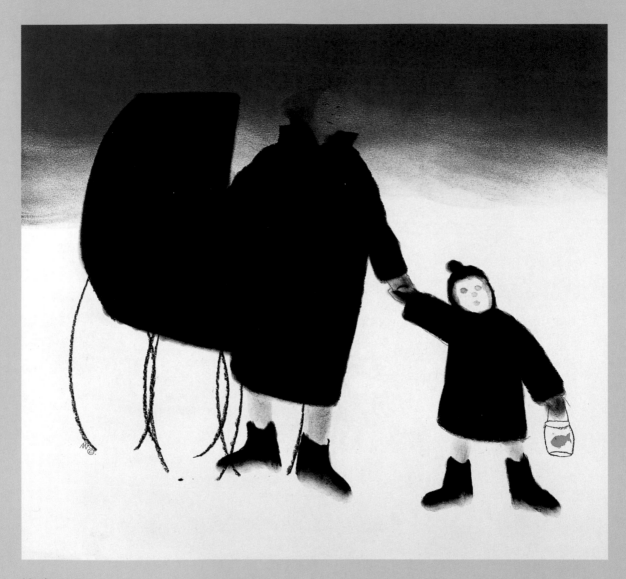

Mother Winter

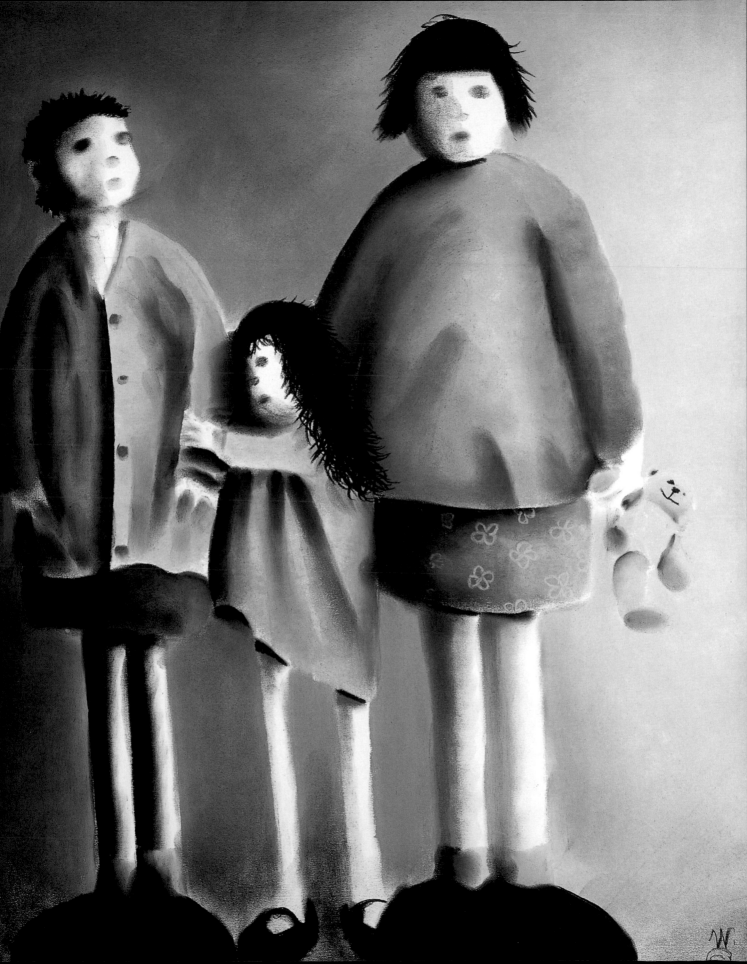

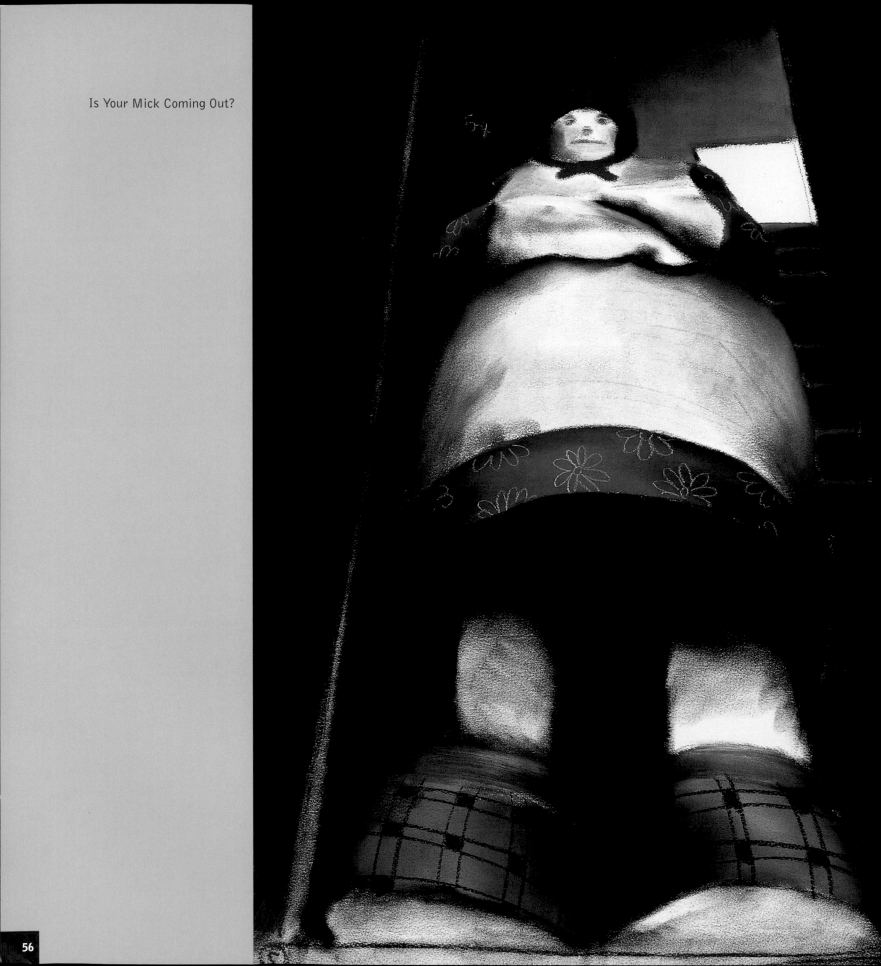

**She filled the door
The house, the world**

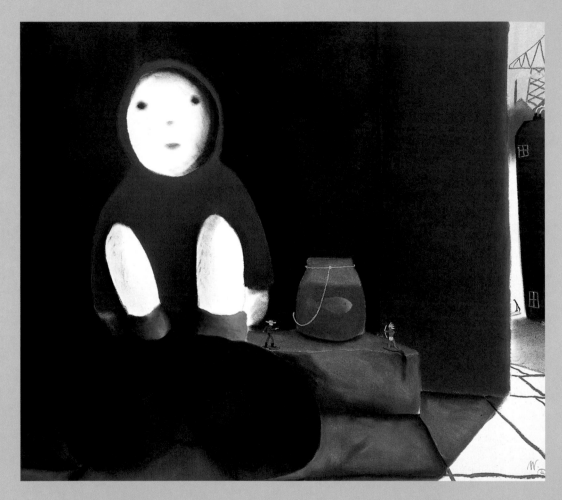

Home of the Brave

FISH IN A GLASS JAR The fragility of the soul is like a fish in a glass jar. You must protect it at all times and know that once your soul is out of the jar it is vulnerable to the dangers of the world.

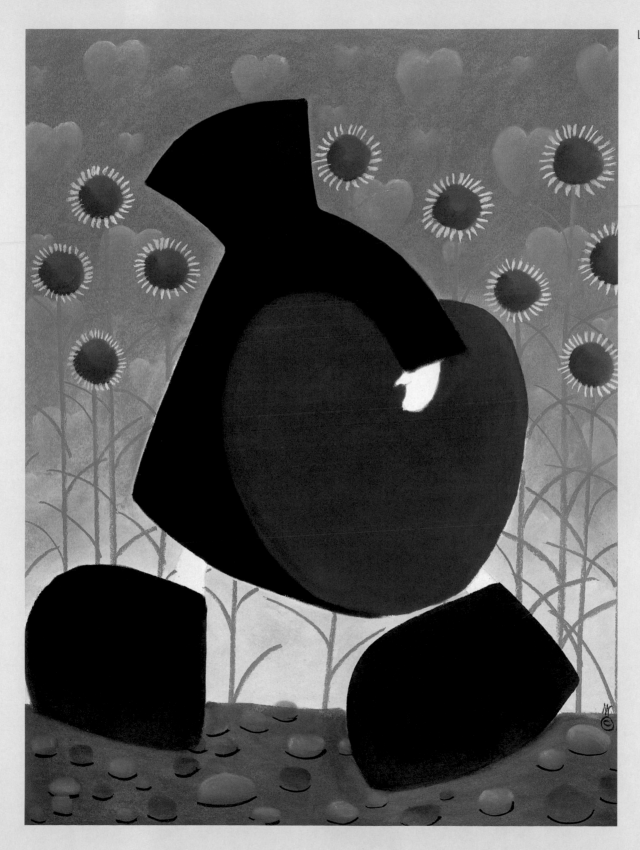

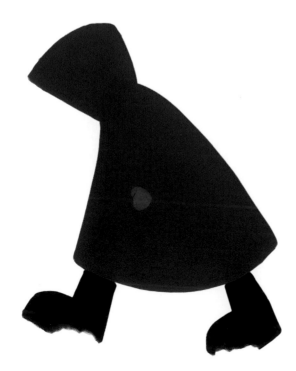

Flying a Kite

First Day in a New World

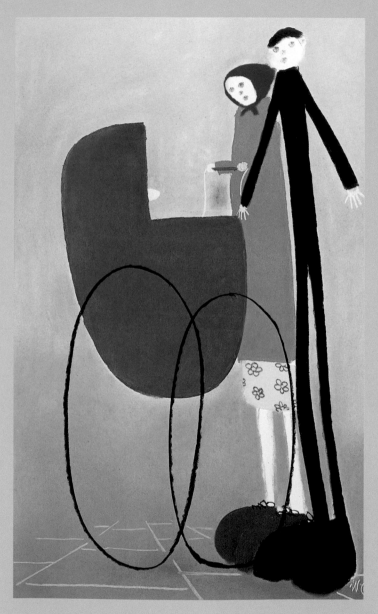

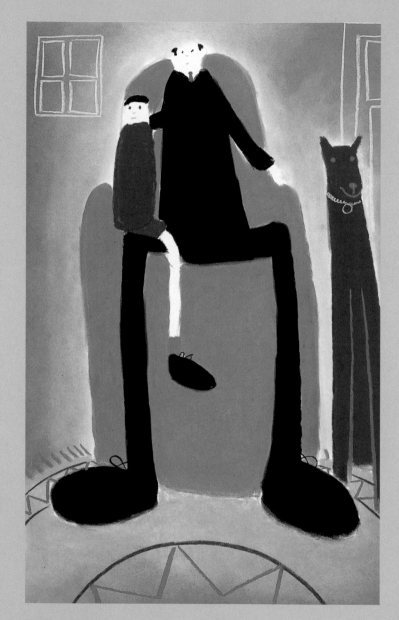

Sitting with Grandad

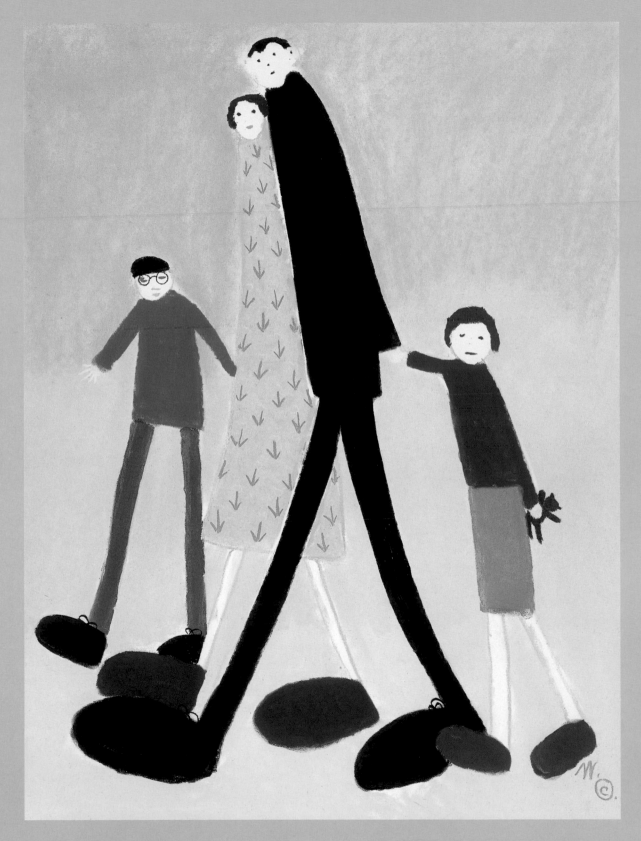

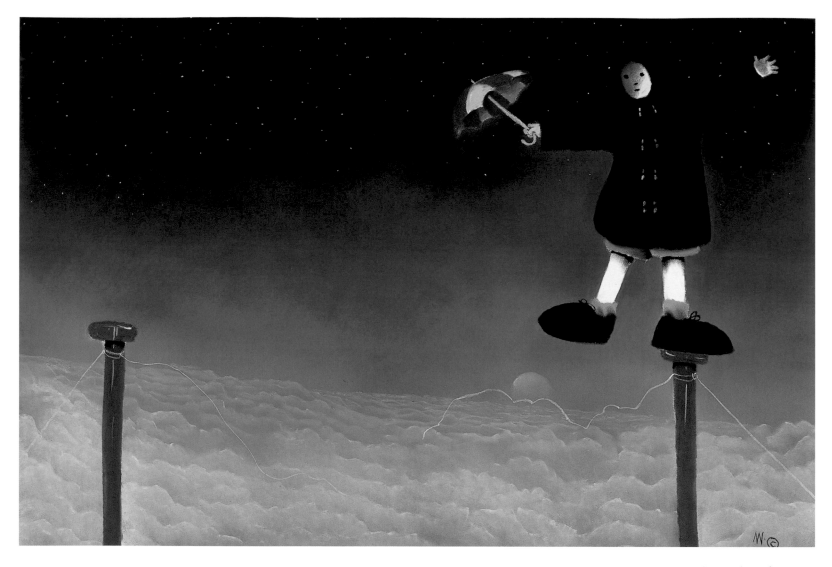

Never Out of Danger

CHILDREN IN DUFFLE COATS Sometimes when I paint a child, he might not have a face. Without a face, he's every child. The cloth of his coat is hardy and plain, his shoes sturdy. Sometimes he has so little, I paint him without a shadow. The landscape is barren, without flowers or trees. The child is totally alone.

But then I might add a bit of color, trying to put some hope in the picture. Because you know that if you invited this child inside, gave him a bath, cooked him dinner, and shared some time with him, it wouldn't be long before you saw the real person within. The child would smile, play games, and talk to you. He'd trust you after a while, his defenses would crumble, and you would see his love and compassion.

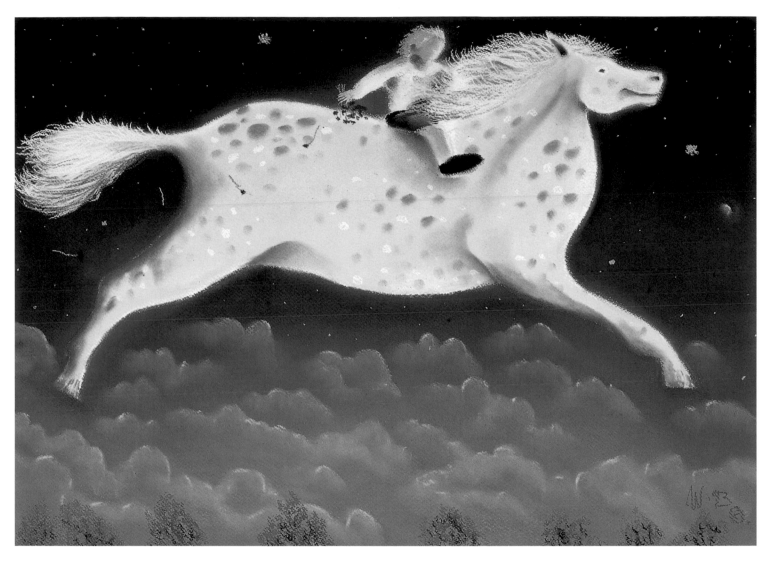

Rider of Love

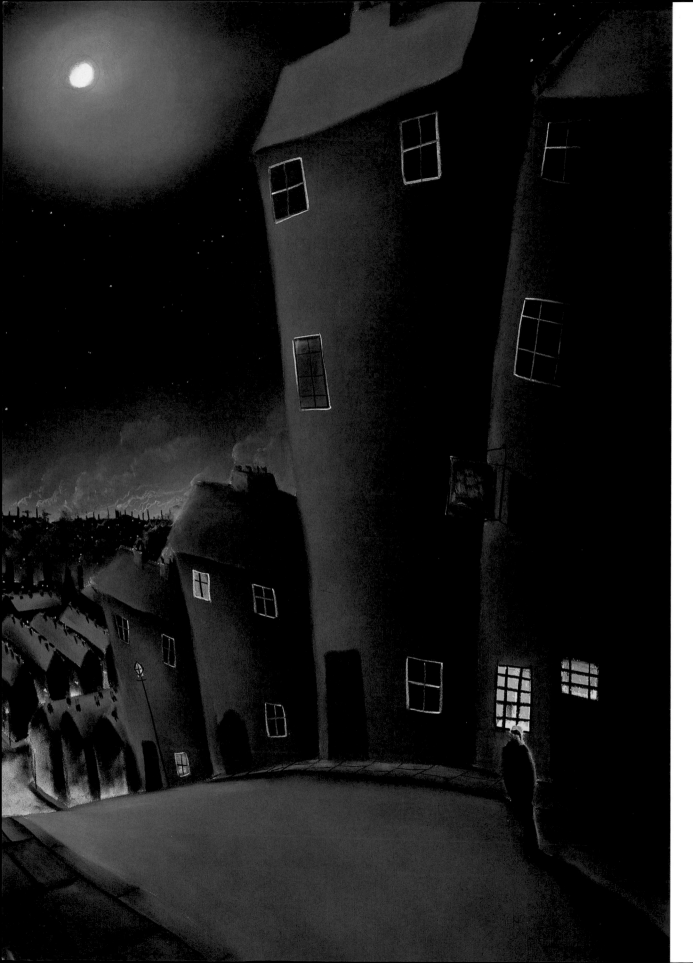

High on a Lonely, Windy Hill

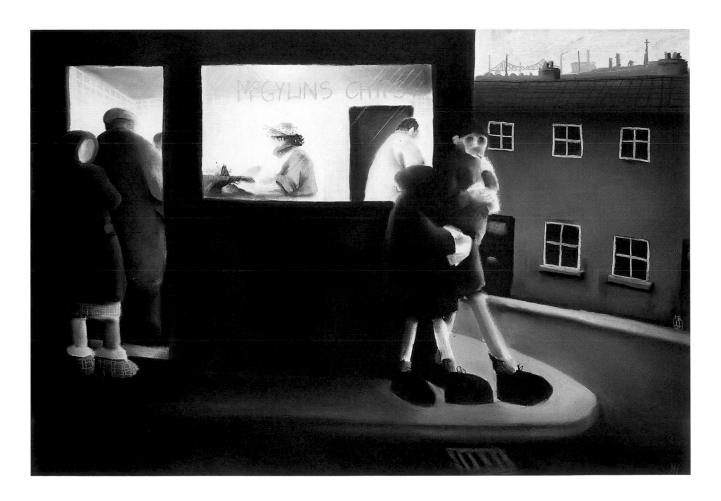

Six penn'orth with vinegar, salt and scraps on…

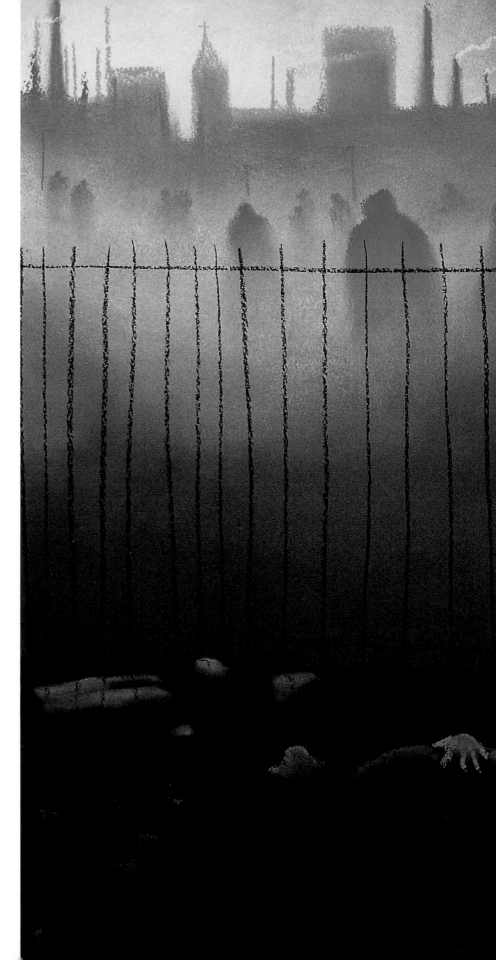

Iveno

**And I shall
Walk the walk
With truth
In my hand**

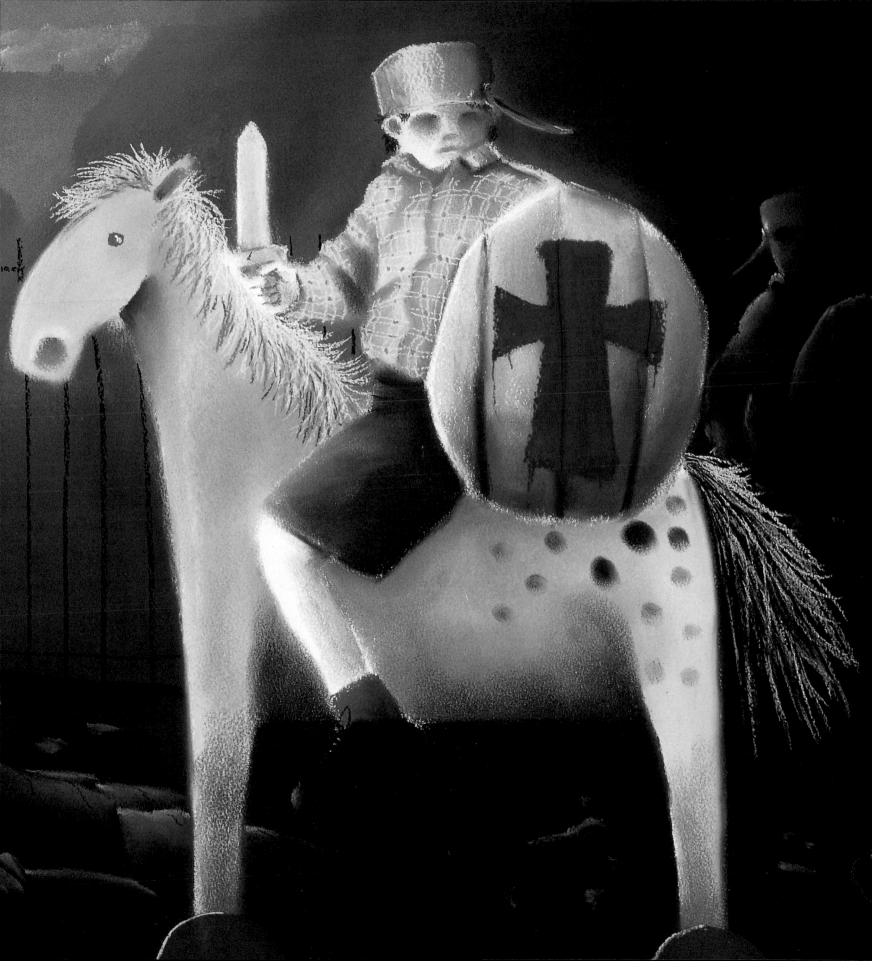

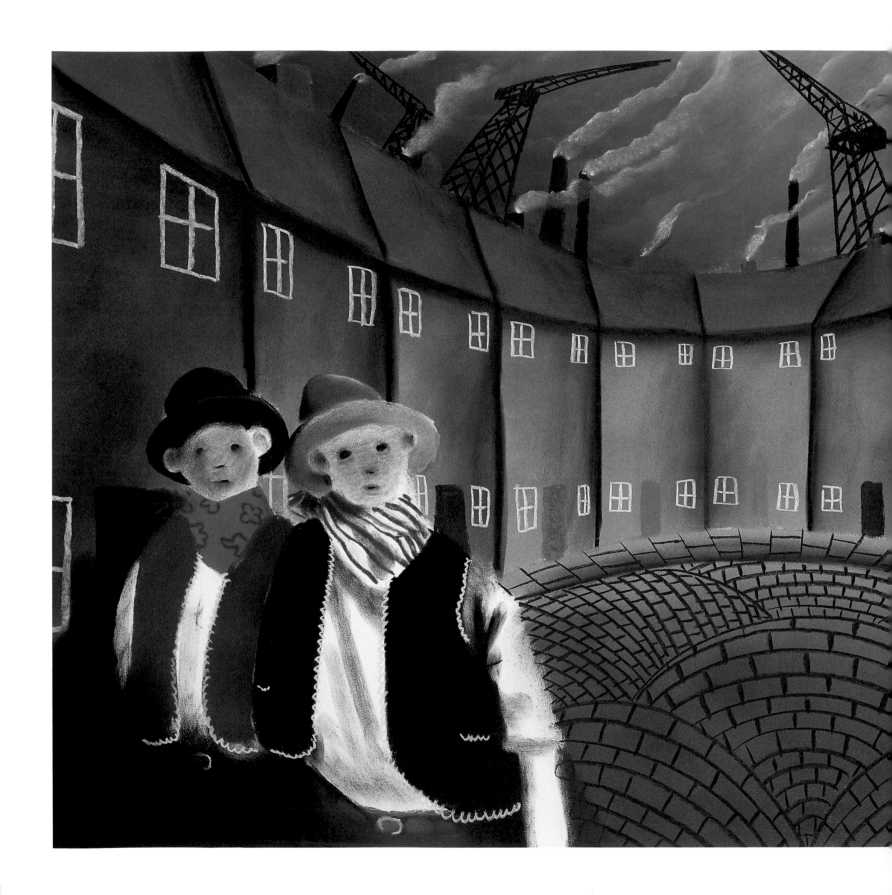

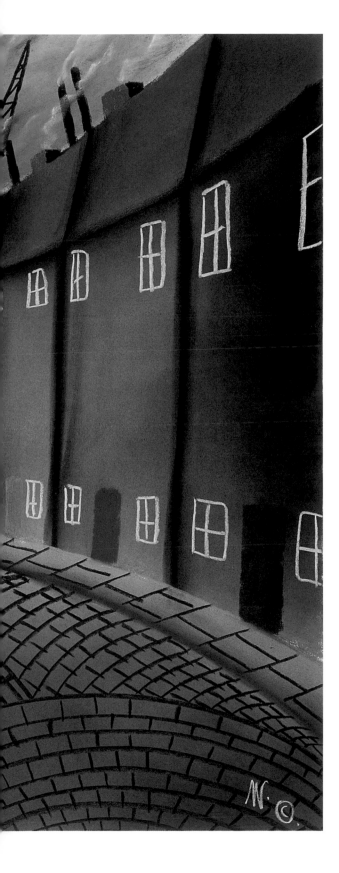

Middlesborough Baddies

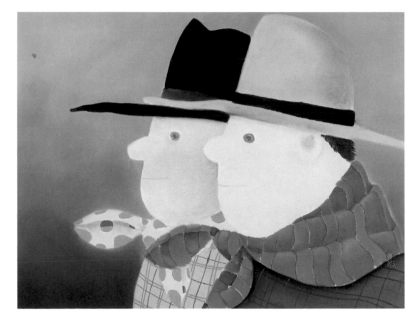

When We Were Young

**Tomorrow never came
We lived in our dreams**

A Parkend Cowboy

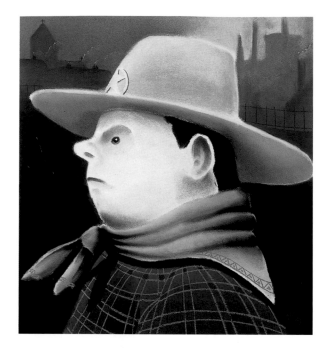

El Gringo

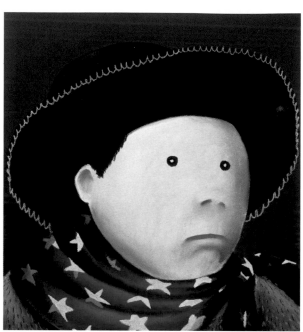

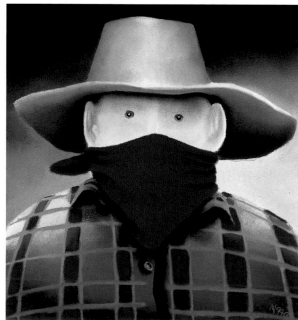

The Outlaw

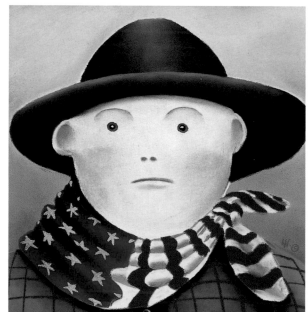

Jake

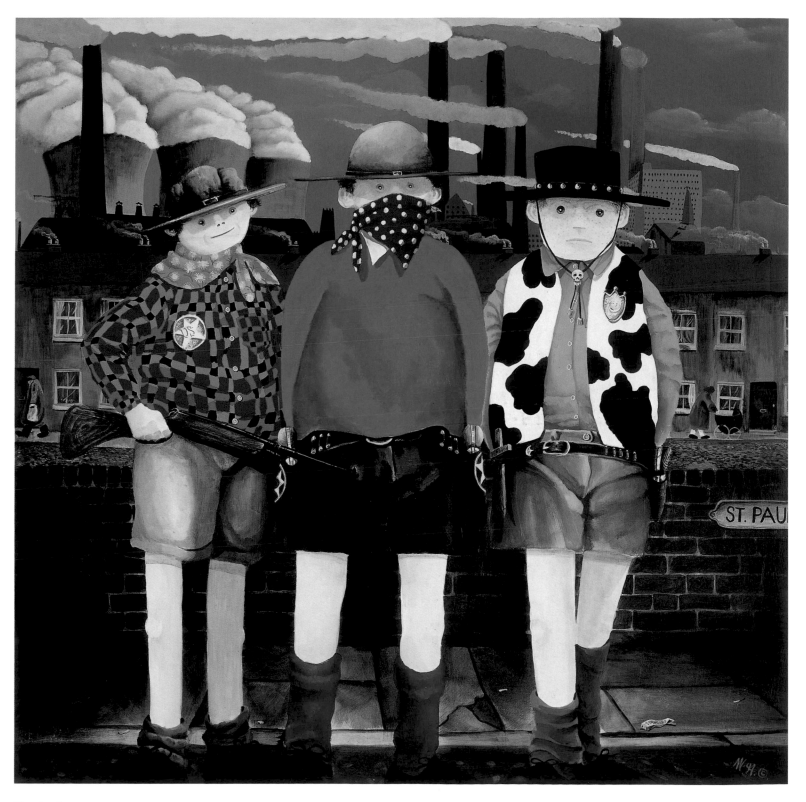

The Outlaw

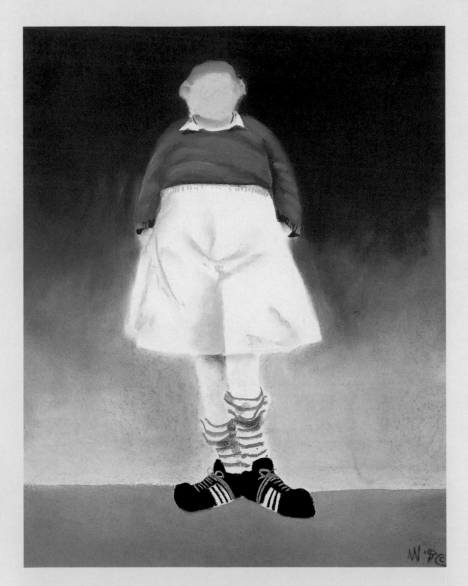

Summer 1965

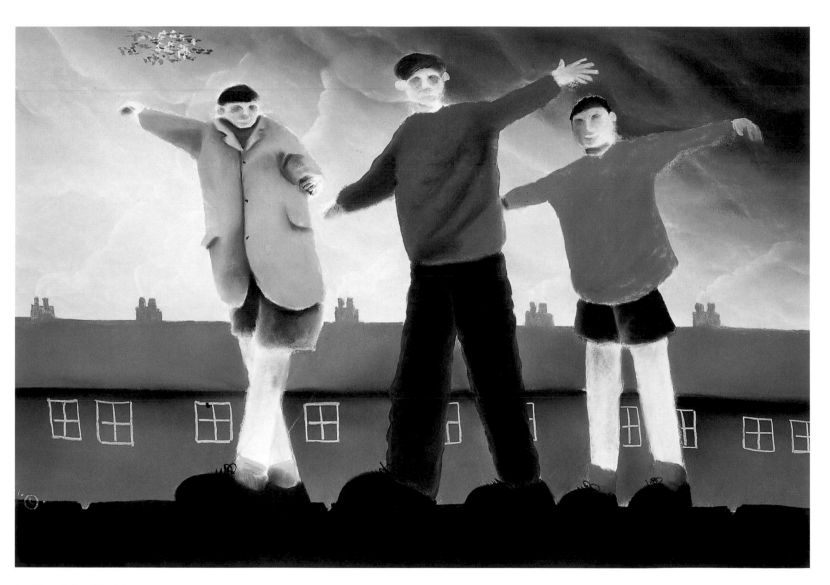

On Top of the World

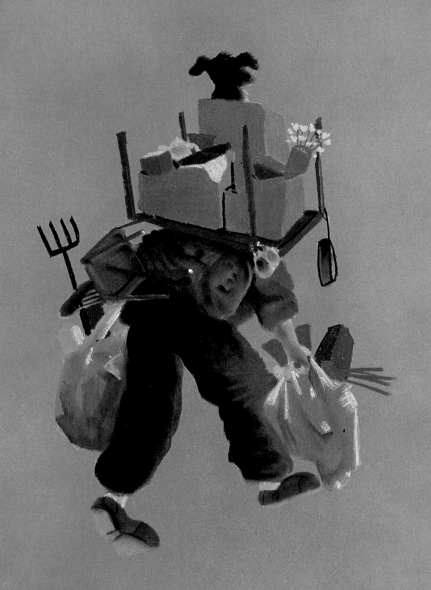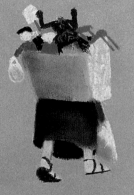

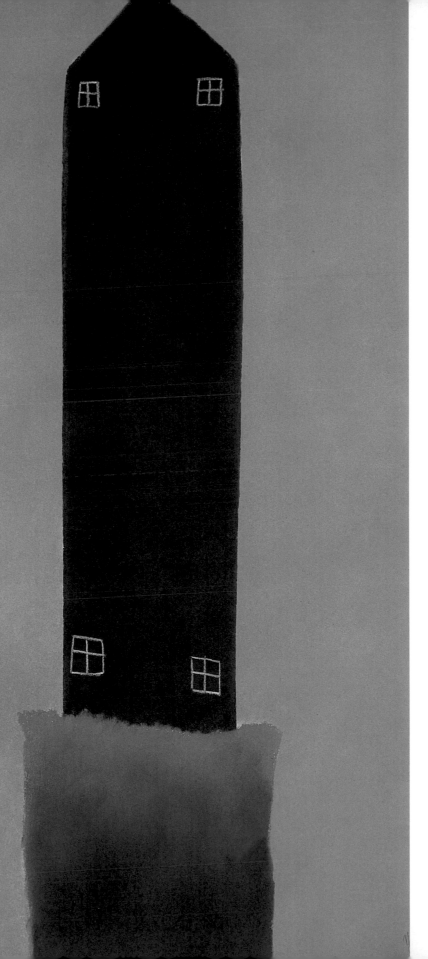

My hometown of Middlesbrough, England, comes through a lot in my work. I'm so proud of it. An outsider might find it hard to be proud of shipyards and steelworks, but I am. I know what's behind that outer layer. When you know these people, when you grow up with them, this is your world. They're your brothers, your fathers, your grandfathers. When I was a child I would see my Grandad going out to work in the morning, and coming home in the evening, tired and dirty, and I would sense his pride. Early in the morning I would hear the sounds of the baker delivering bread, the van's tires on cobbled streets, the greetings exchanged: "Morning George." Late in the evenings, I could hear the sounds of men singing in the distance, sometimes arguing, their bellies full of ale, opinions strengthened by the effects.

I draw and paint the streets of my hometown, but they really could be anyone's. We all have our memories, those warm nostalgic feelings that wash over us, when we remember with fondness.

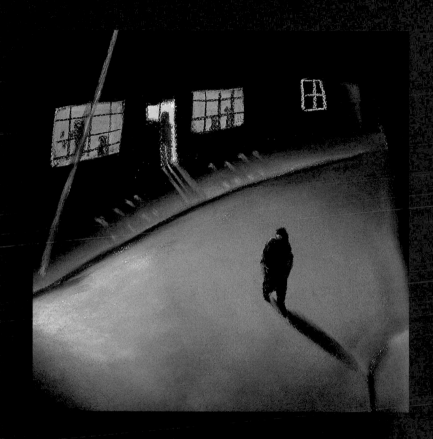

Heading Home

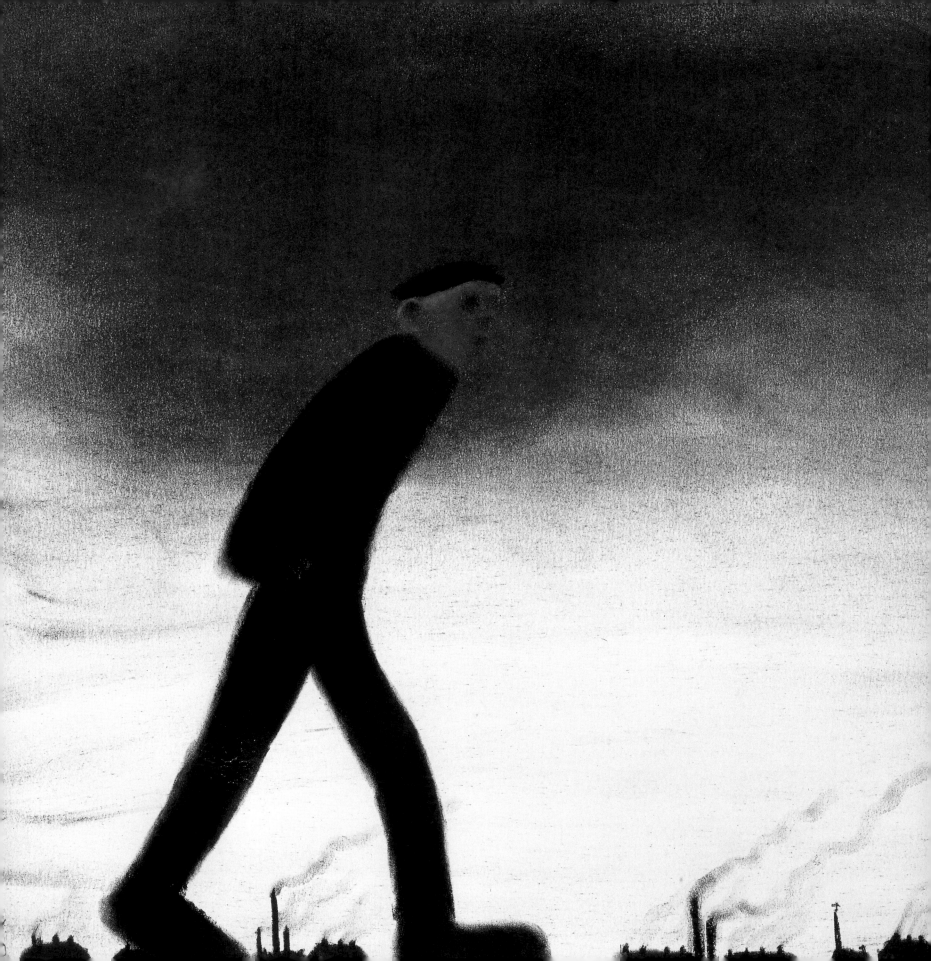

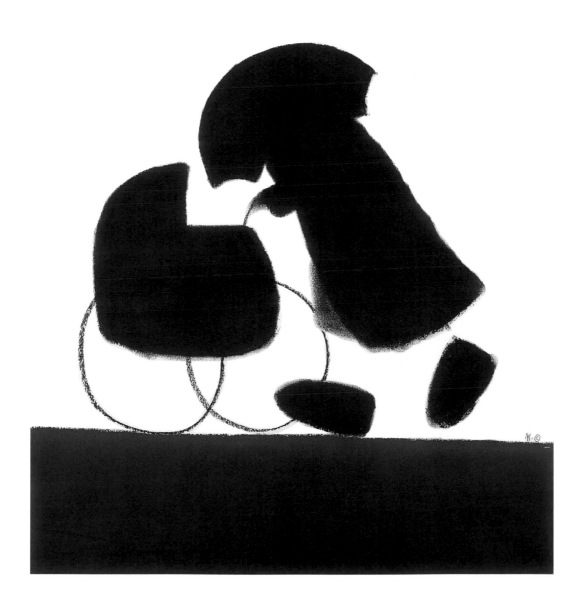

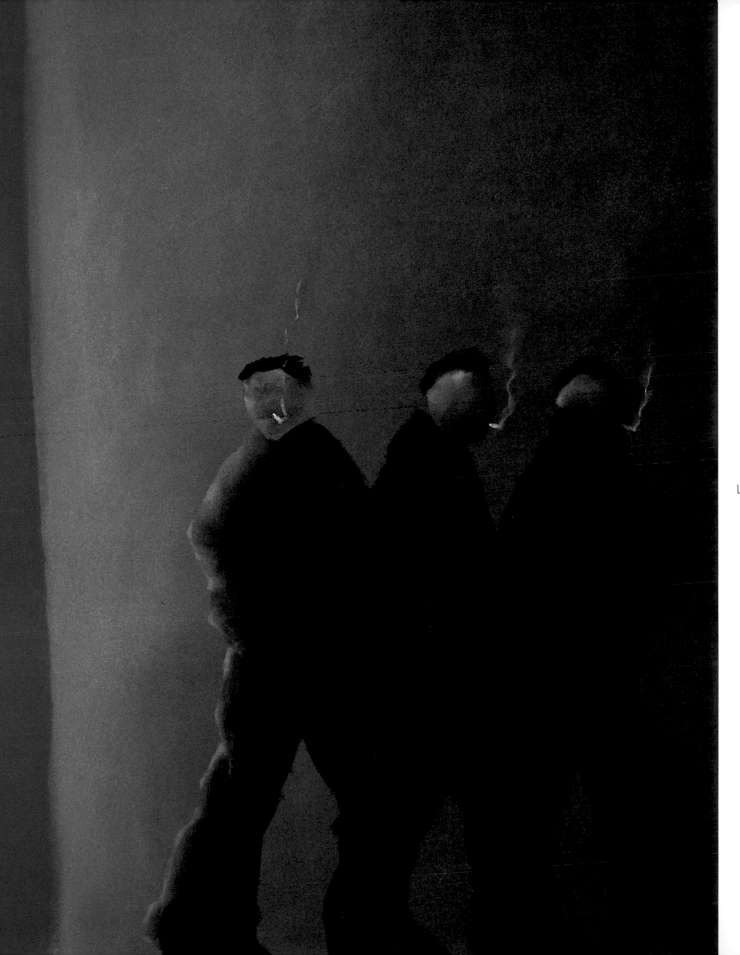

Left for Dead

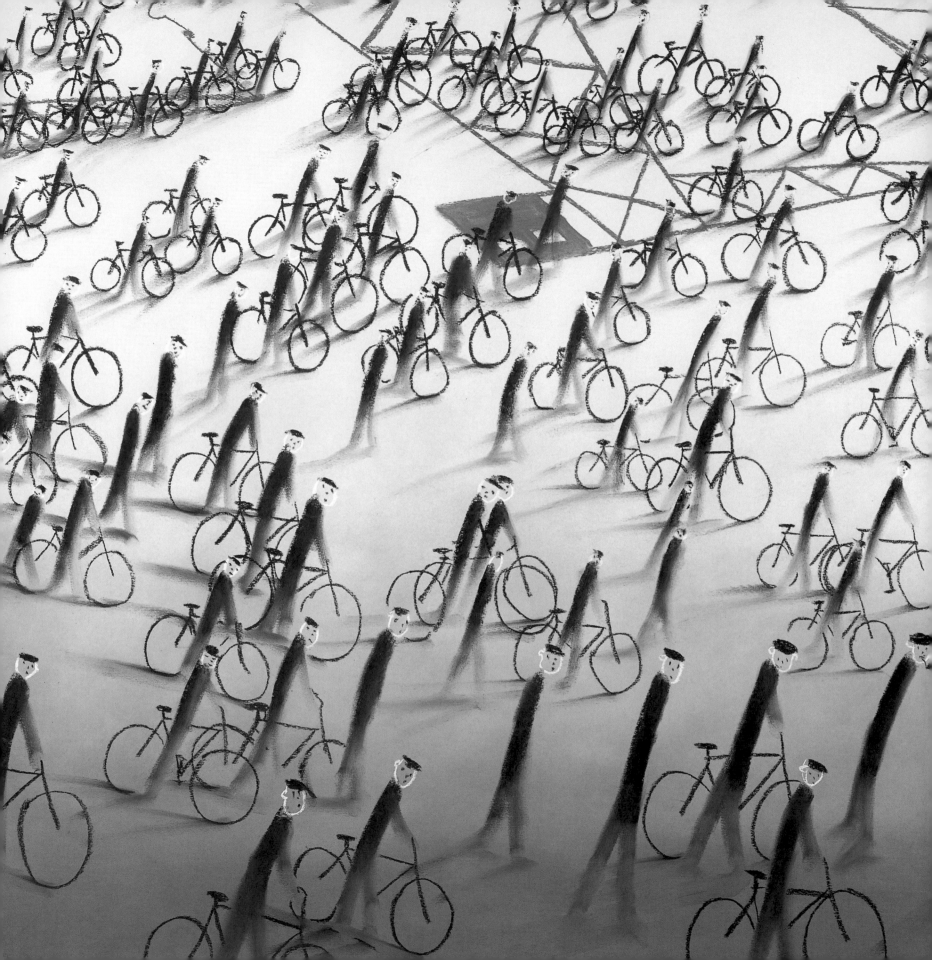

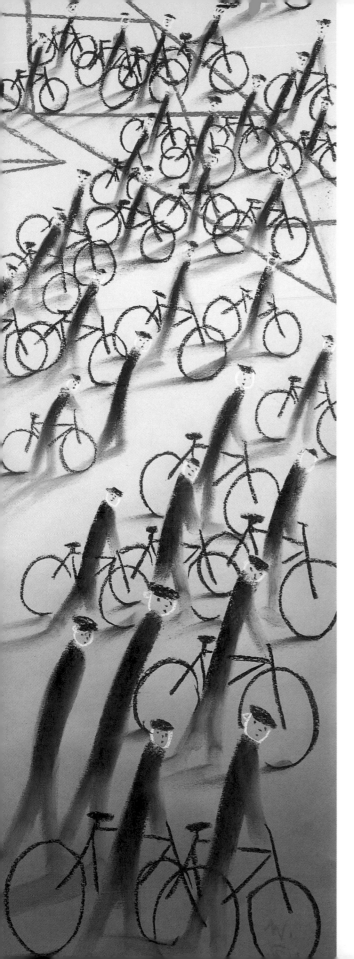

In the Sound of the Siren

WORKING MAN With some of my paintings, I'm building a monument to the working men who no longer have jobs. The ships aren't built in my town anymore; the steel and iron have gone. The men are now unemployed. I'm putting that precious history down on canvas.

I want to capture the passion of when they did work: the molting of the metal, the sound of hammers on steel. There was a pride, a beauty in these men. Their lives were hard, but they worked even harder and were valued and had a sense of purpose. Now some of these proud strong men have not had a job for twenty years or more. Their heads hang down, they don't use their strength, their arms. In some of my work you will see their arms are gone, unneeded.

It's tragic and cruel— these men want to work but the jobs are no longer there for them.

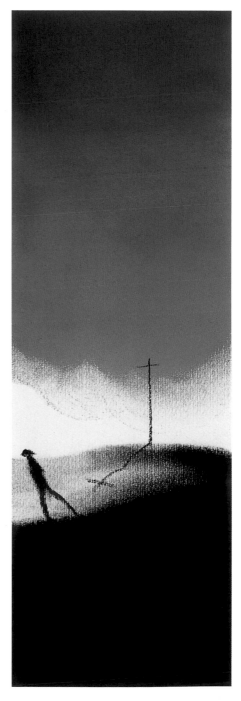

Towards Home

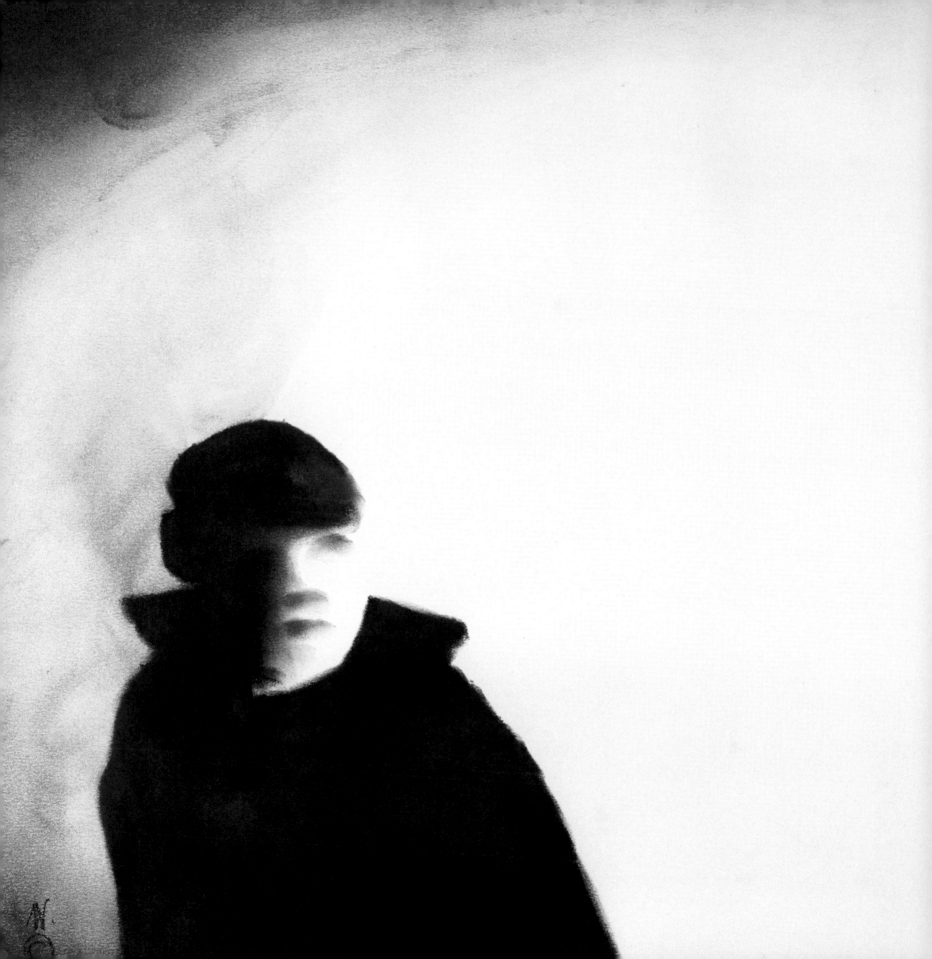

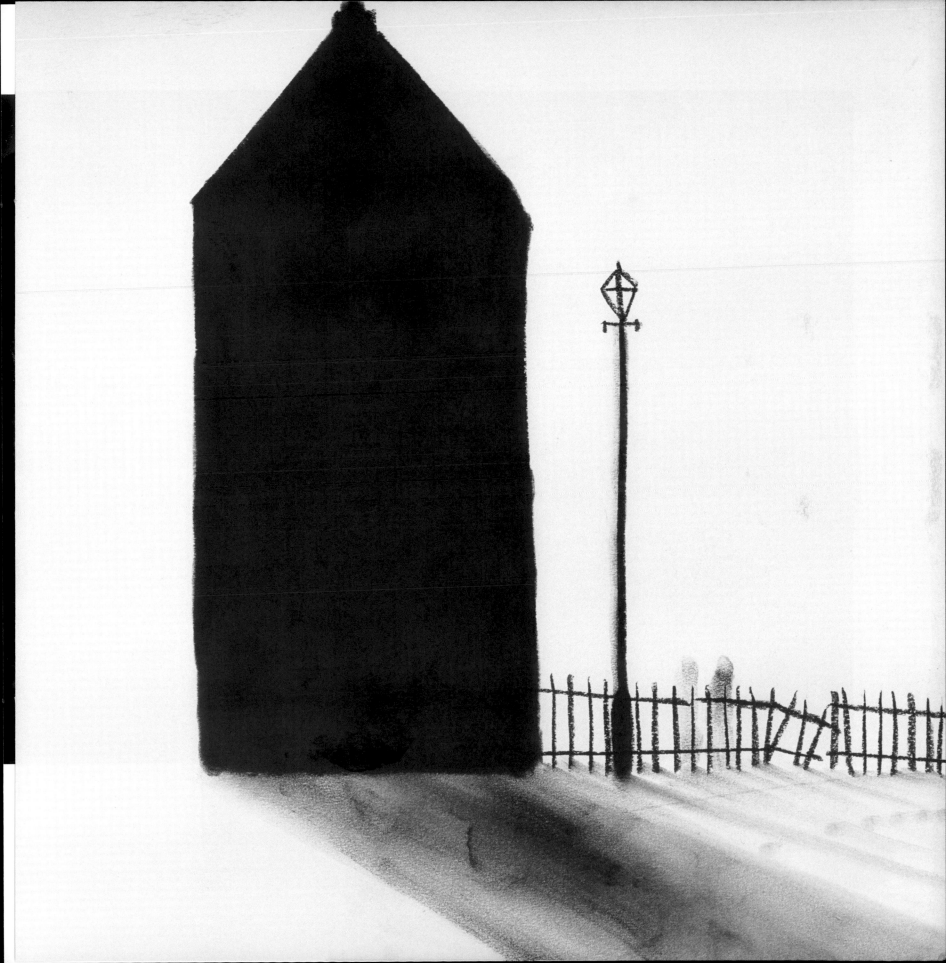

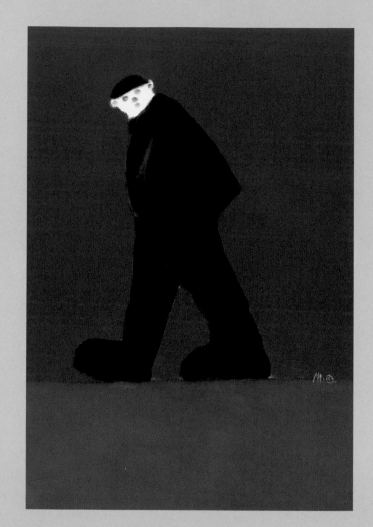

On His Way

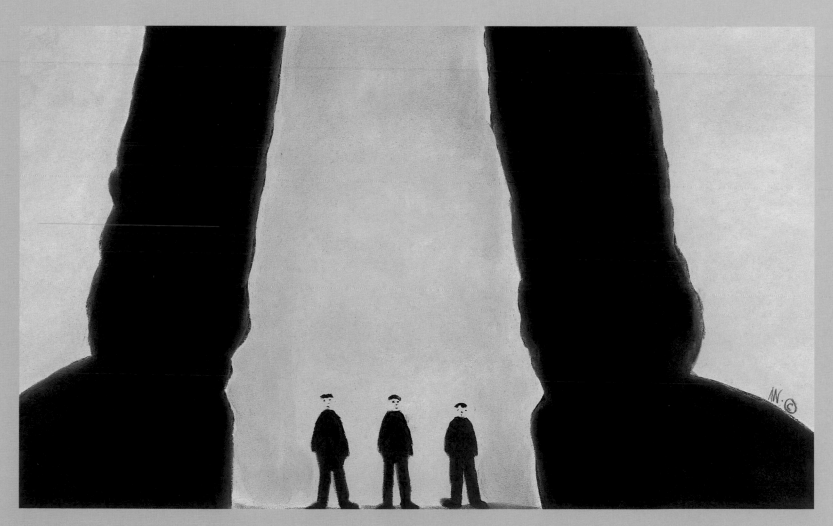

Middlesborough Stand Off

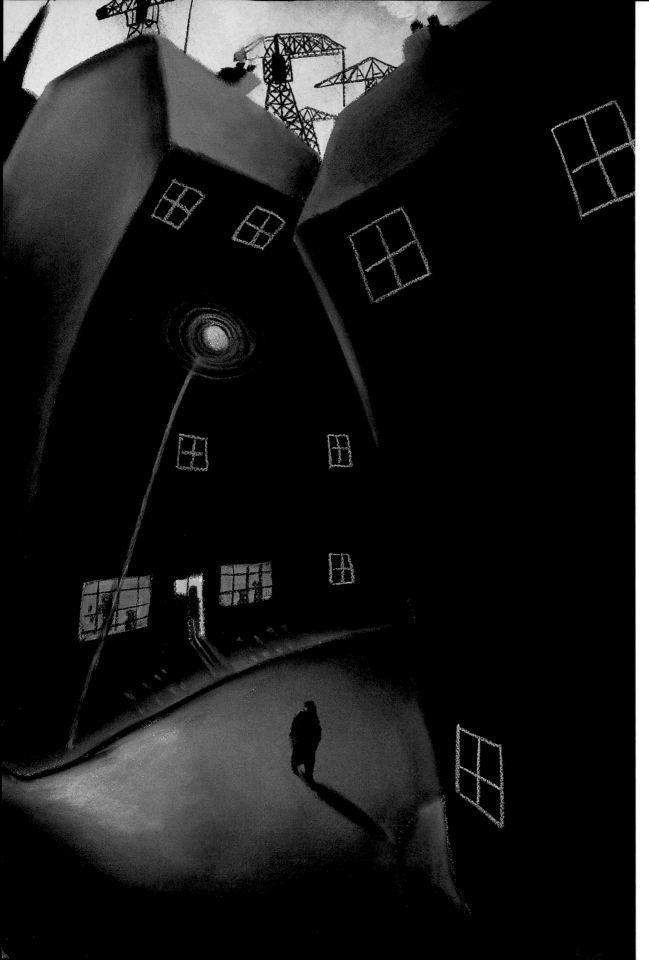

Time

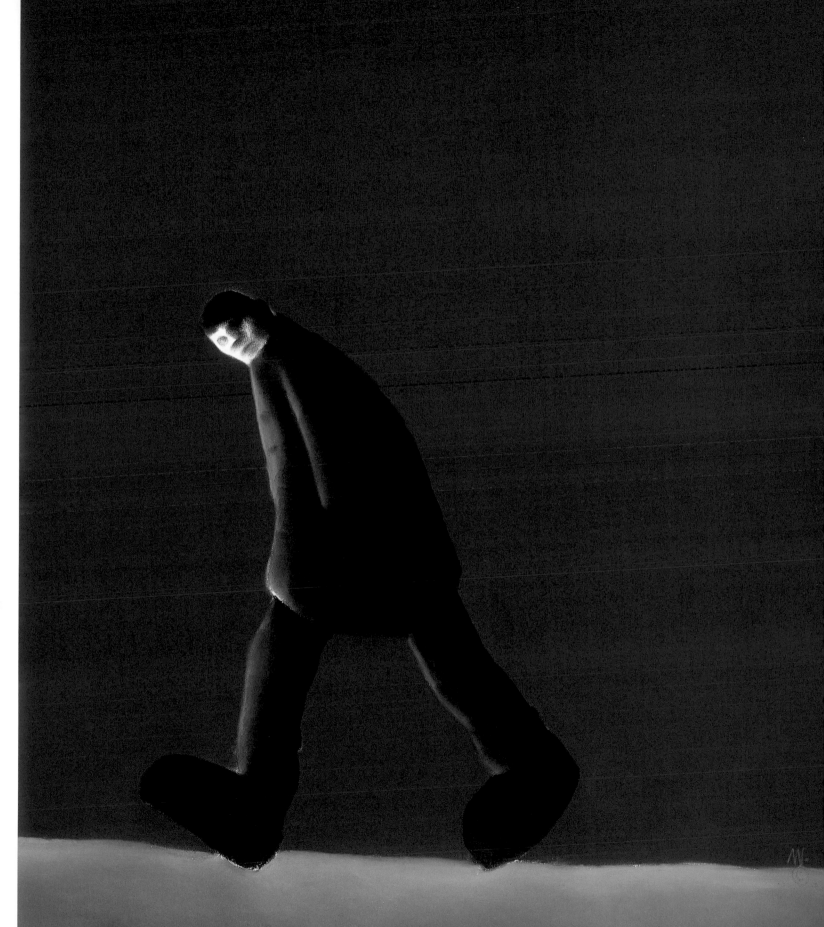

Hell Frozen

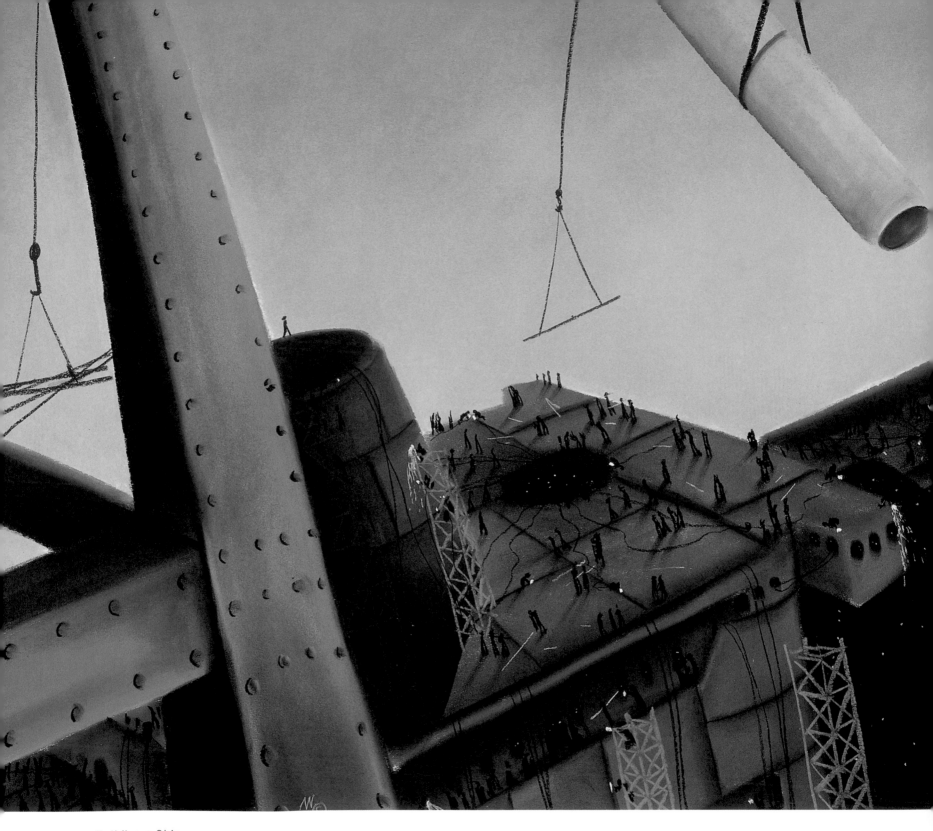

Building a Ship

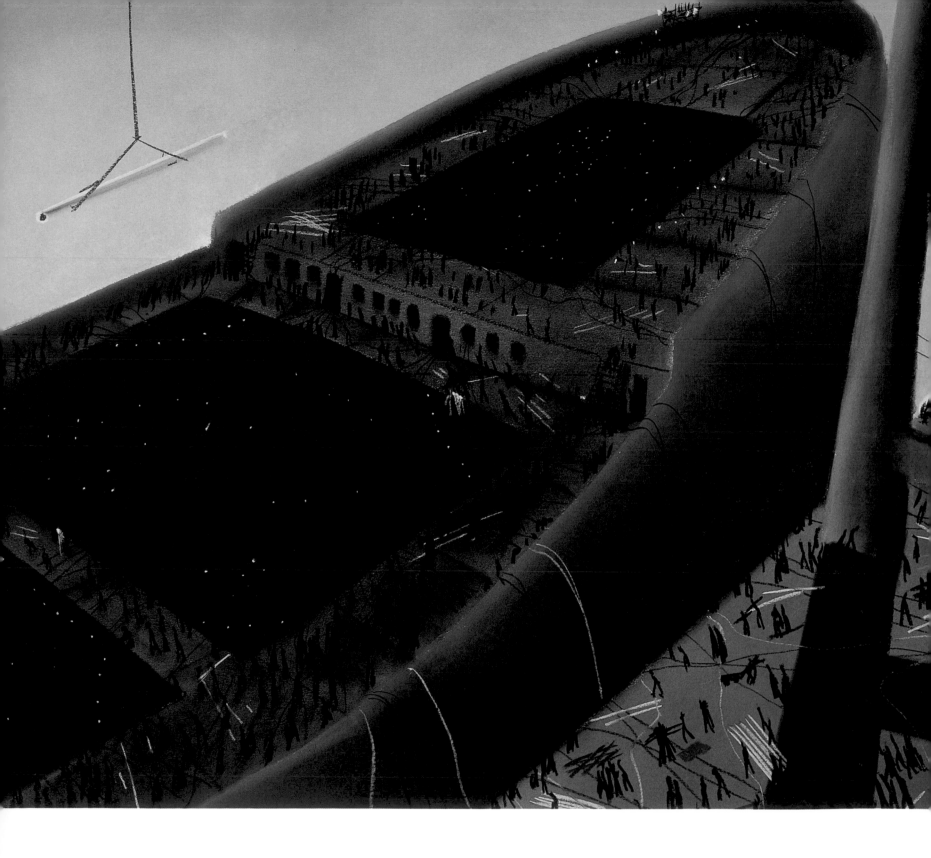

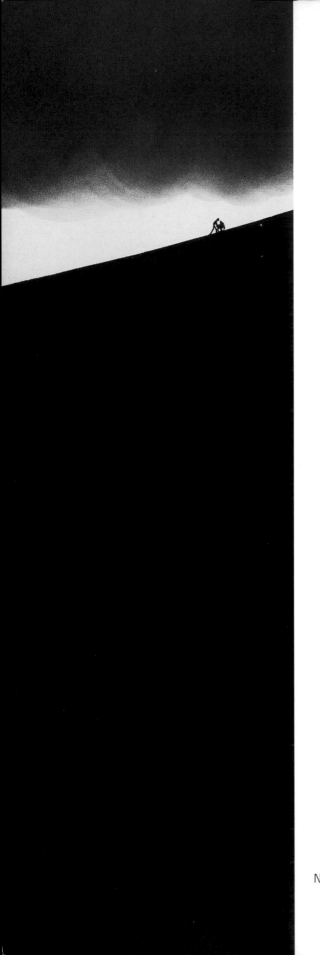

Nearly There   A Kiss to See Me Throu

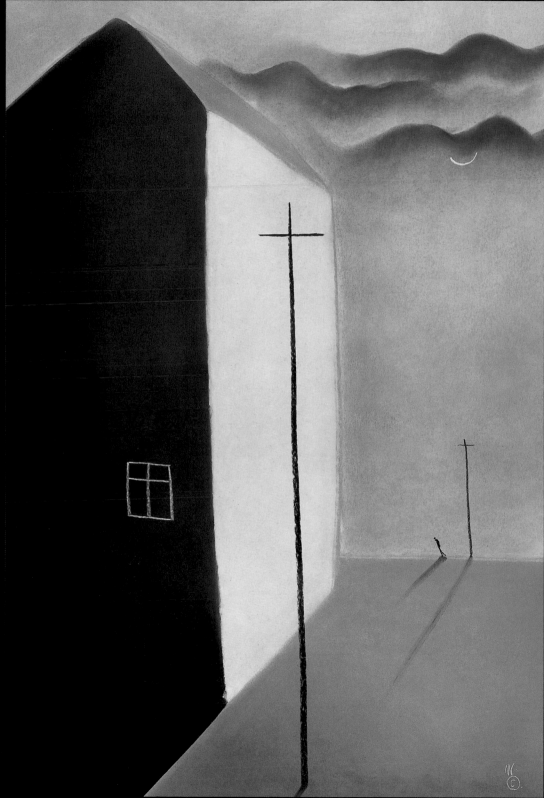

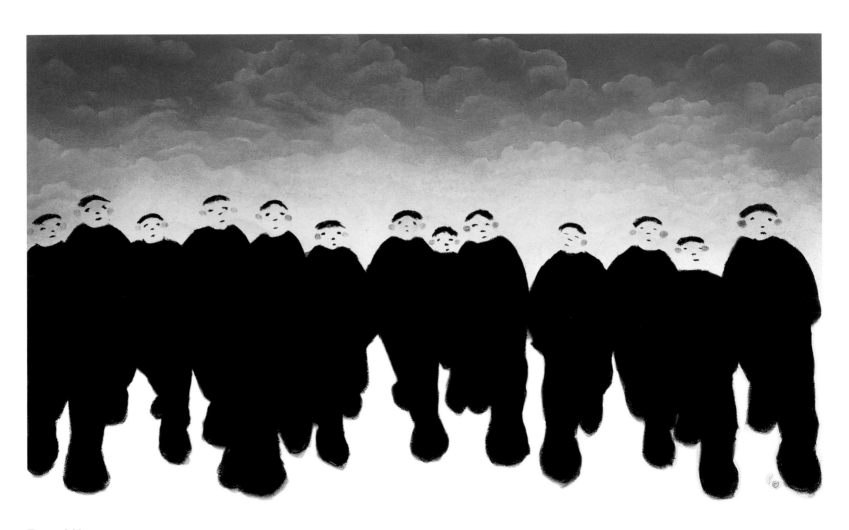

Toward Me

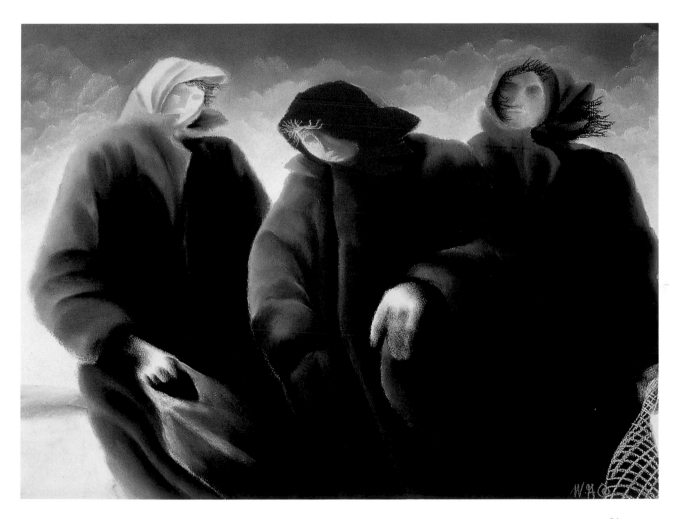

Shoppers

Overleaf
It Was Shrouded in Darkness

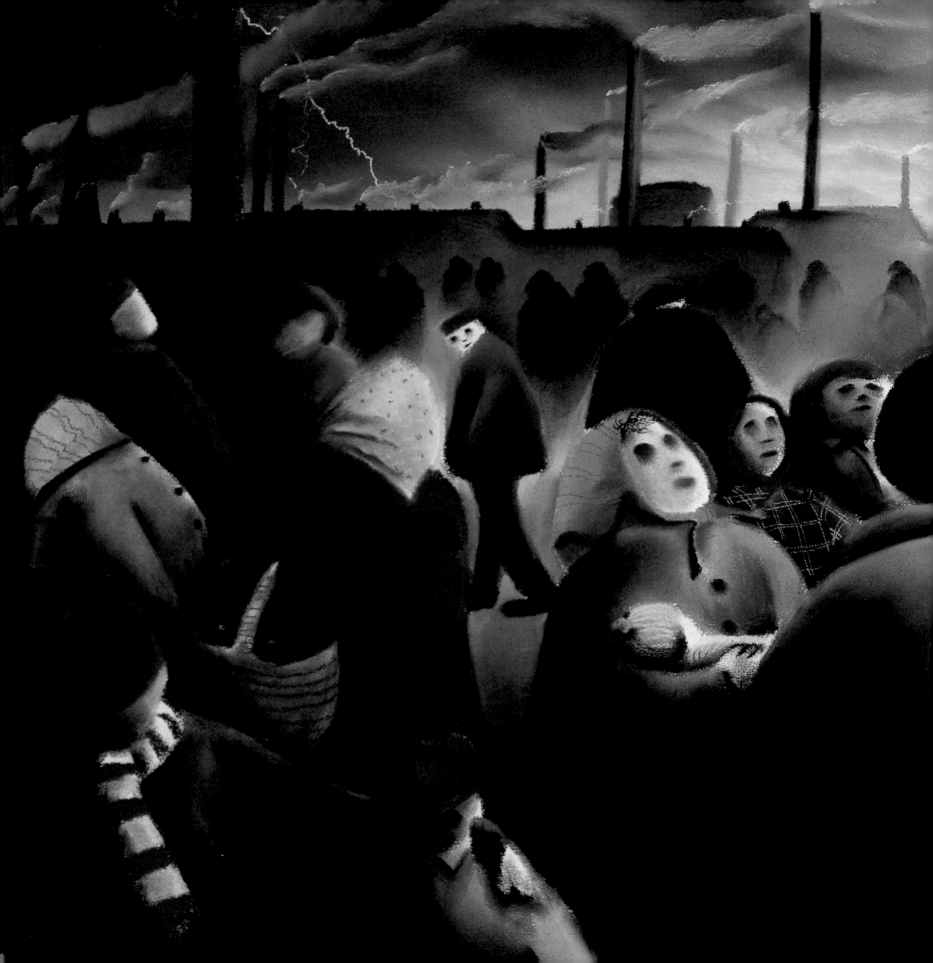

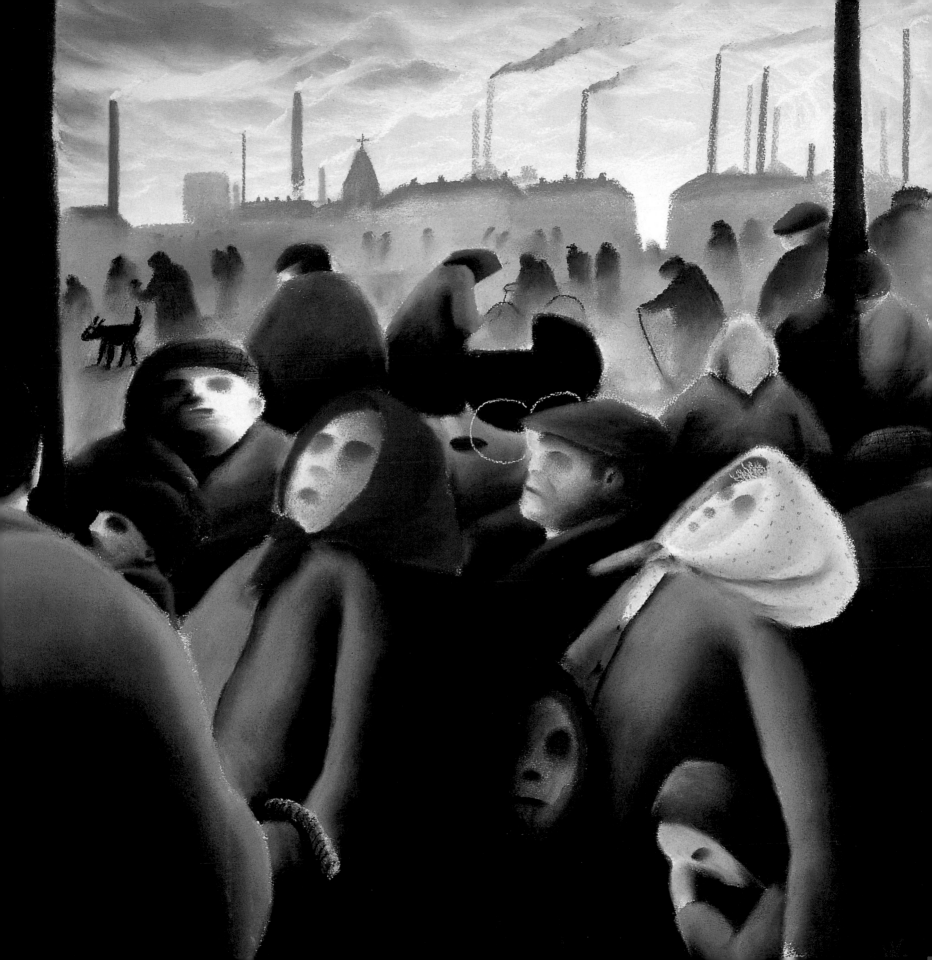

For me, love is the most important thing. Nothing else comes close. All of the riches in the world cannot compare to the love I share with my family. Sometimes I will draw children surrounded by flowers, smiling and happy. These images are symbols of the sheer joy and love of life, for the innocence and beauty and hope I see all around me. It is a source of strength and pride to me and it's there for us all.

Like a delicate flower, love can be easily crushed through purpose or neglect. Yet still, in the hottest desert or the highest mountain, a flower will find a way to grow. No matter how you cover a seed, the flower will find a way to survive. You can't stop it from growing. And if you put it in a nice pot with sunshine and water, you'll end up with a bush which will grow and blossom, leading to many flowers.

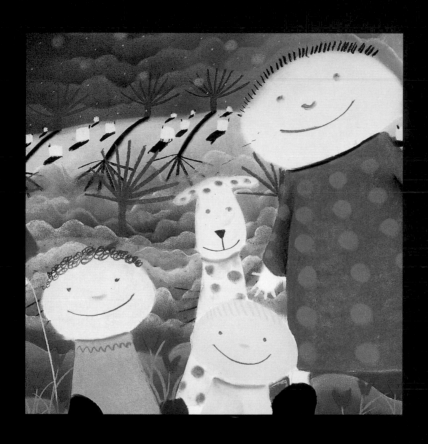

The Loved

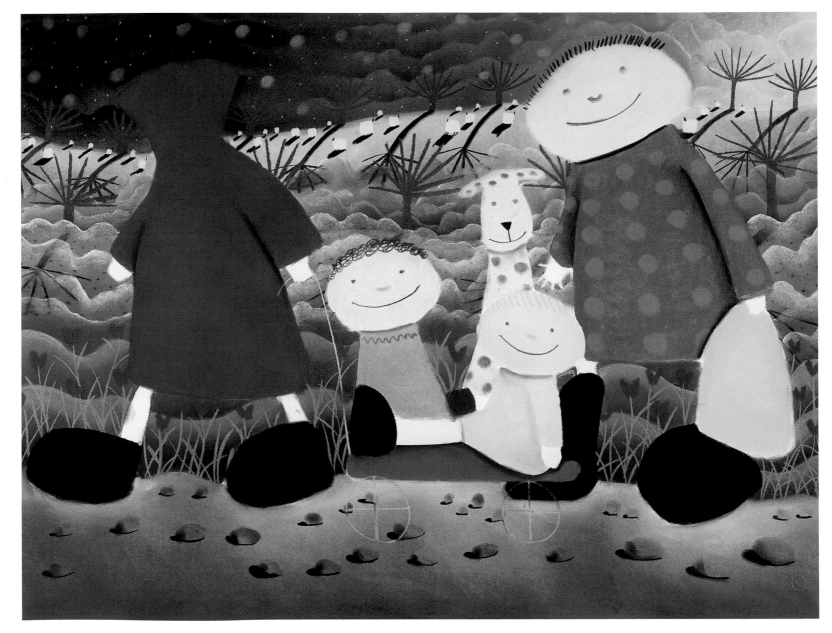

Taking Them Out

Of a smile

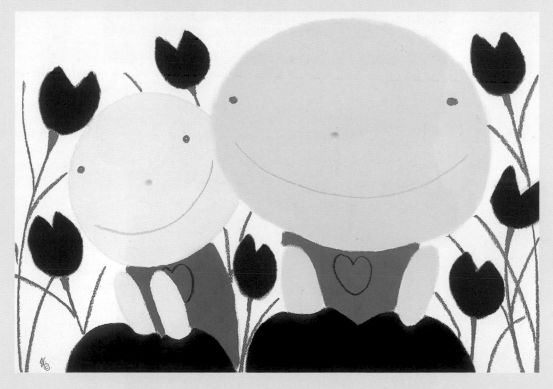

Self with John

BIG FEET The big feet symbolize that I never want to forget where I came from, no matter how different my life has become. It can be dangerous to forget your roots. Your ego takes over, and you've got wings on your feet. If I got too full of myself, I wouldn't be the man Susan fell in love with and married. I wouldn't be the father of my children. My feet are firmly planted on the ground, and that's where I want them to stay, totally grounded. It's important never to become bigger than your shoes.

The Lovers

The Searchers

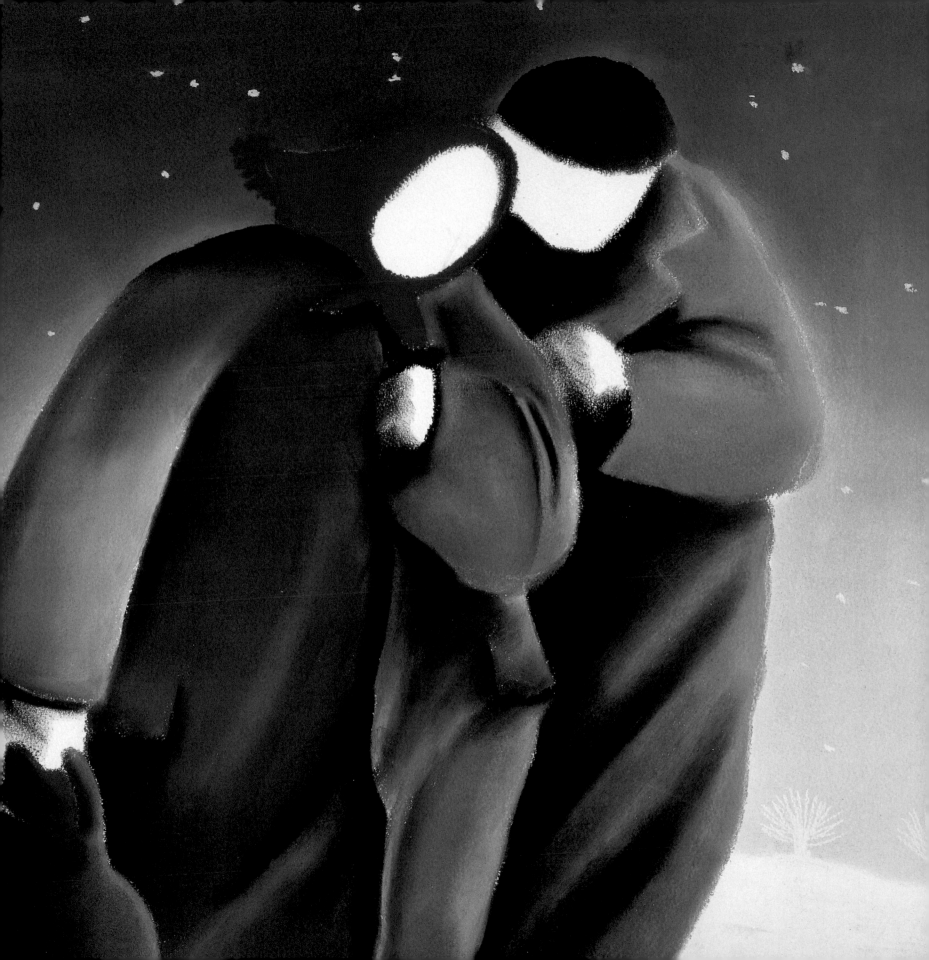

Flowers for Christmas

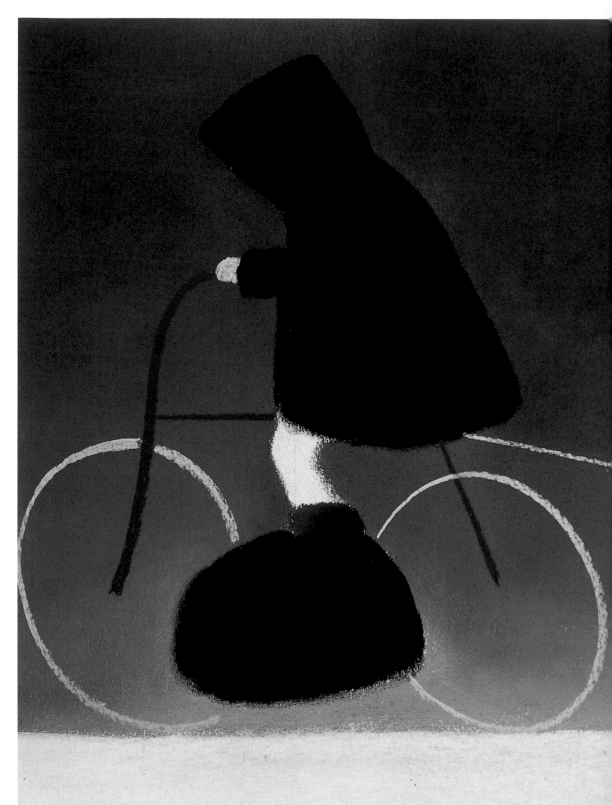

And through the snow

he brings you

his

Love

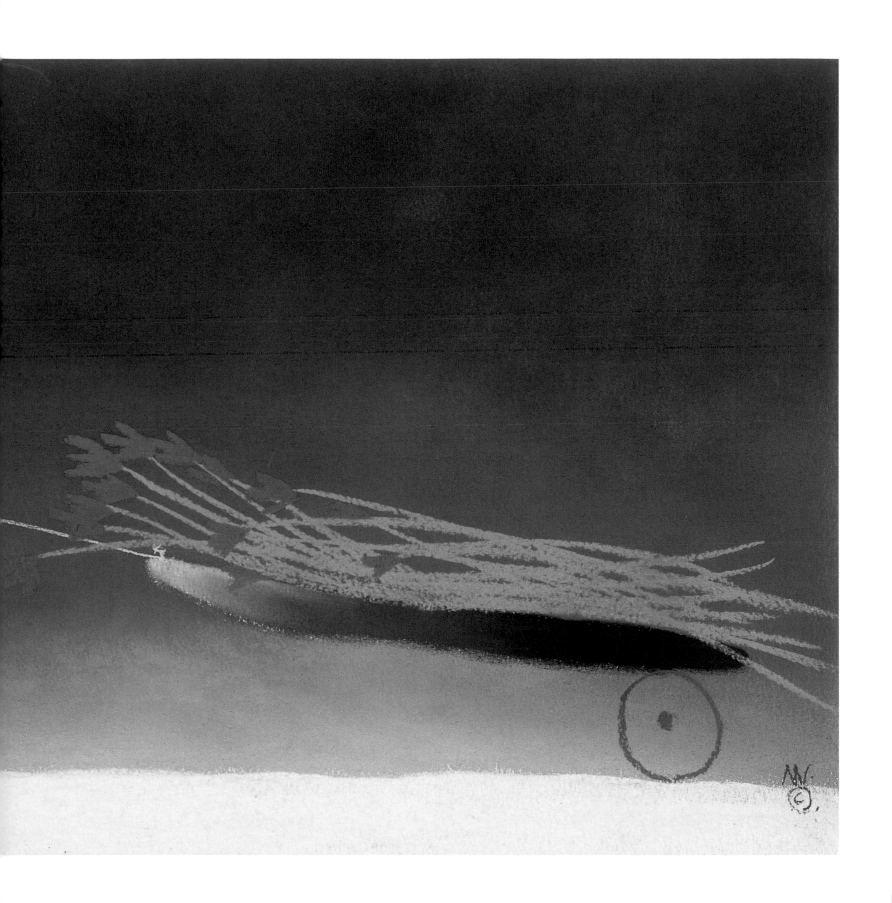

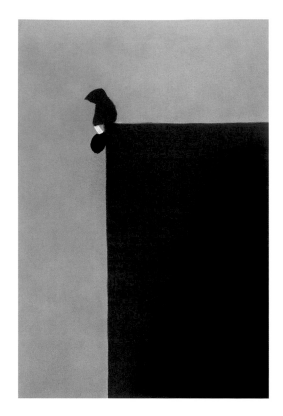

Sitting

CLIFFS There have been many transitions in my life, like when I decided to pursue my career as an artist. My family comes with me to the edge of these new experiences and together we look over "the cliff" and know that everything will be just fine.

The Ecstasy

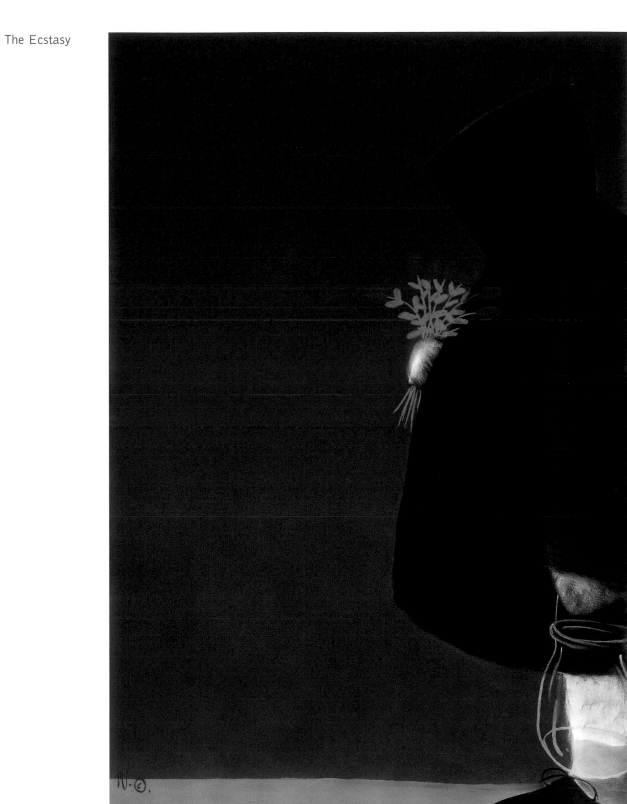

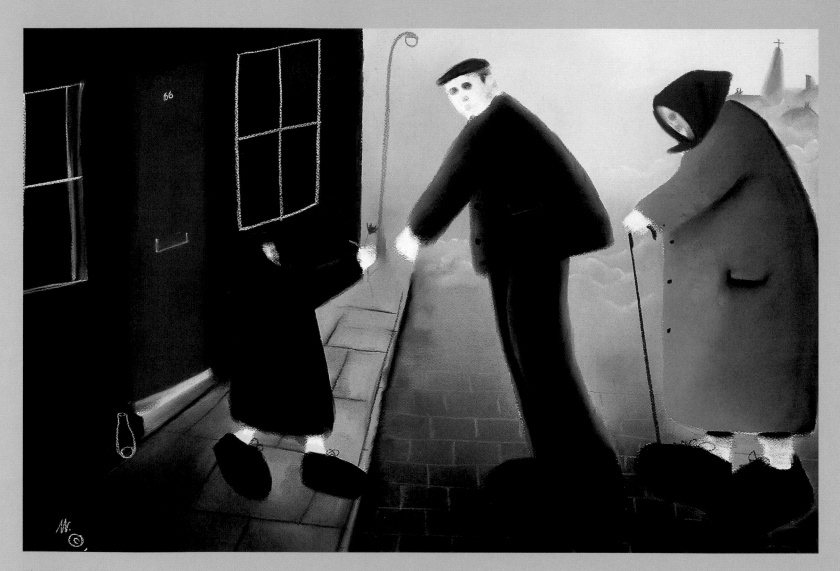

The Visit

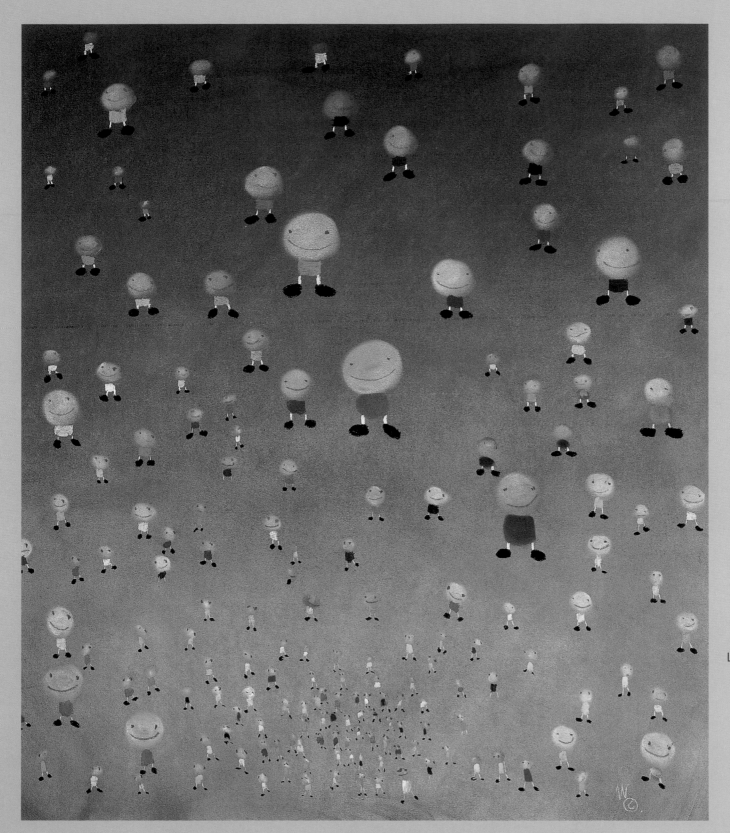

Lost and Found

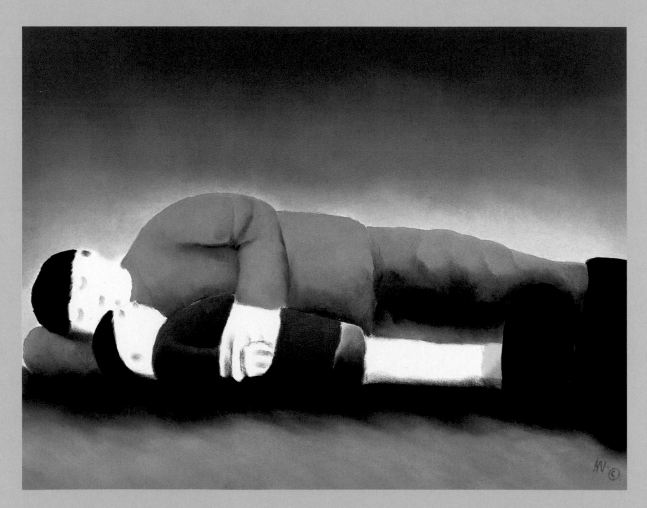

Return to Me

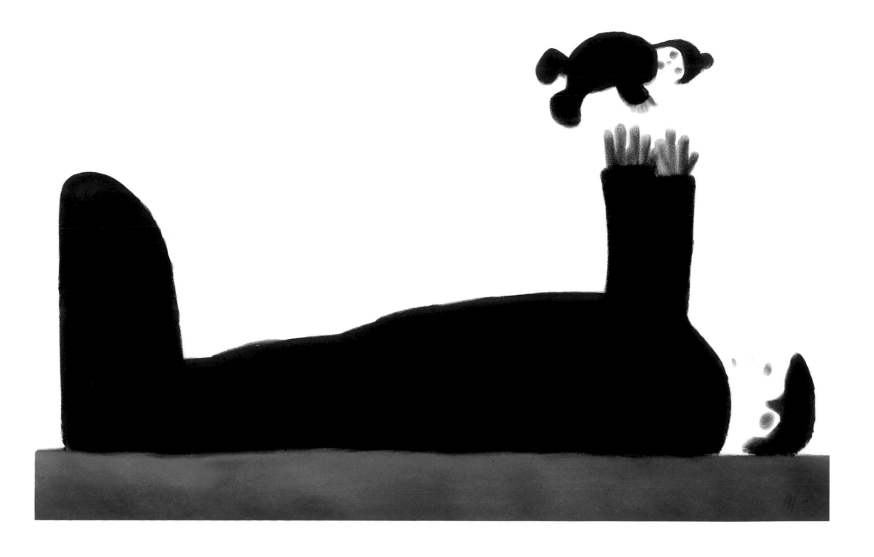

I try to bring hope with my art. We all have hopes and dreams, which we should hold on to, because they tell us what we really want in life. No matter how big, how wild, how outrageous our dreams are, they can point us in the direction that is going to give us fulfillment and happiness. Everyone—from lawyers to laborers—faces life's challenges. Most people have gone through some form of hardship and some have grown as a result. In all of hardship there is a glimmer of light; it may be very small, but it's there. I want people to laugh and I also want them to know it's okay to cry. By remembering our struggles we can see just how far we have traveled.

Sometimes my life has been a dark tunnel, but a productive dark tunnel. You've got to do your best to come out at the other end. All sorts of things have happened in my life, but I'm here, I've survived. I have hope and joy and it's there in my work.

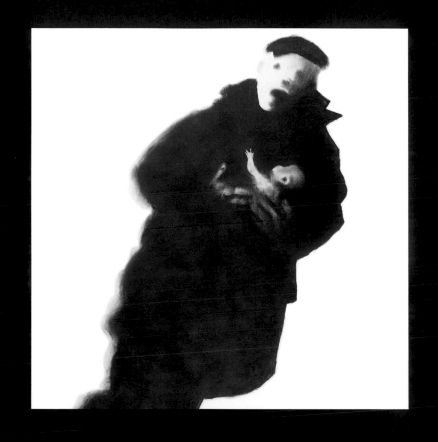

Hope

Don't use words
Nor eyes
Feel

Gloria

The Bud

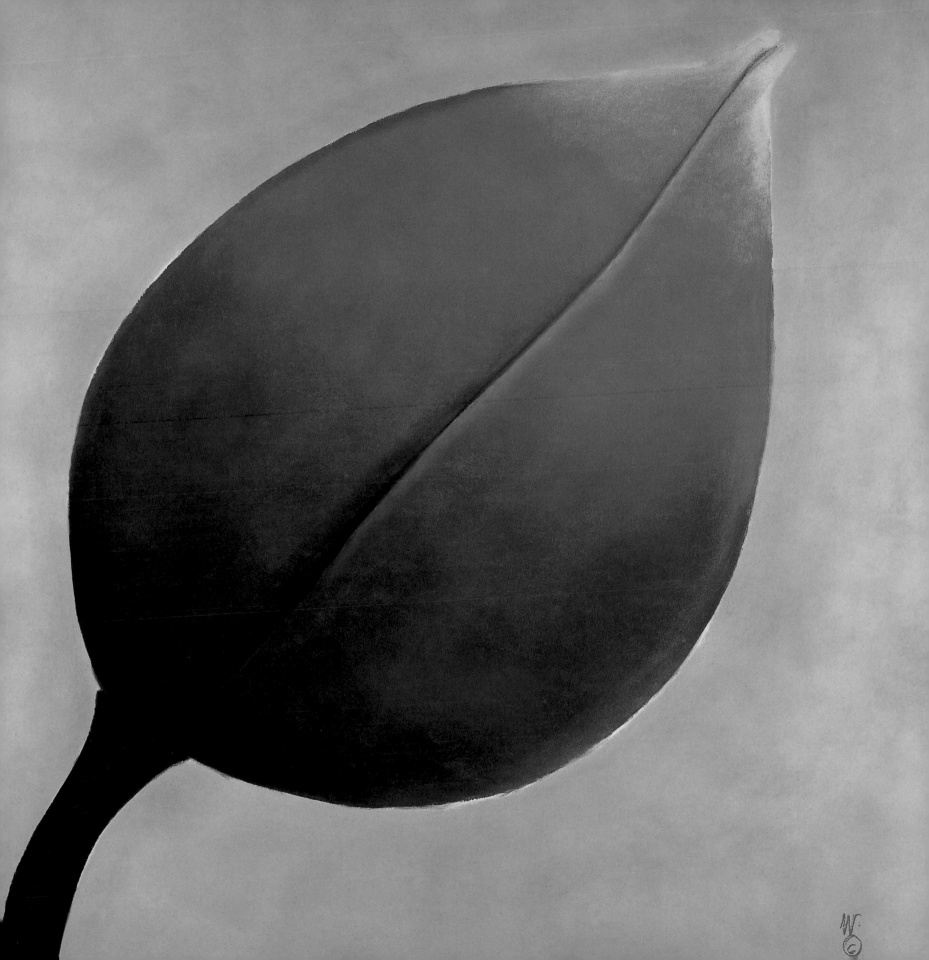

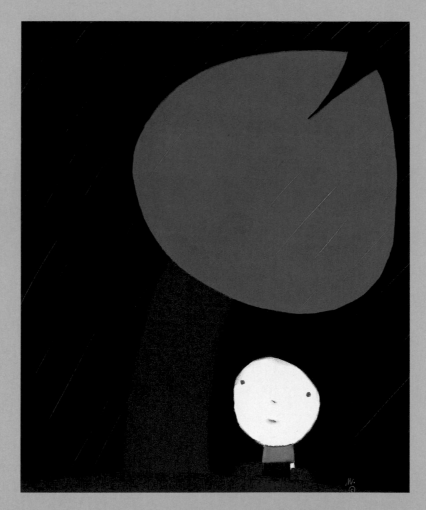

Sheltering

Don't Let Them Down

For some
Hardship ...
But he has
The Beauty

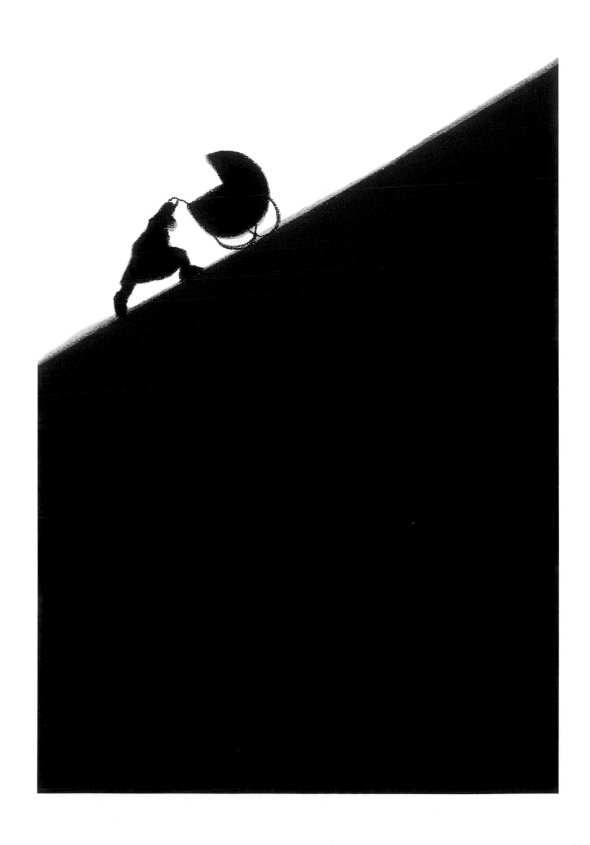

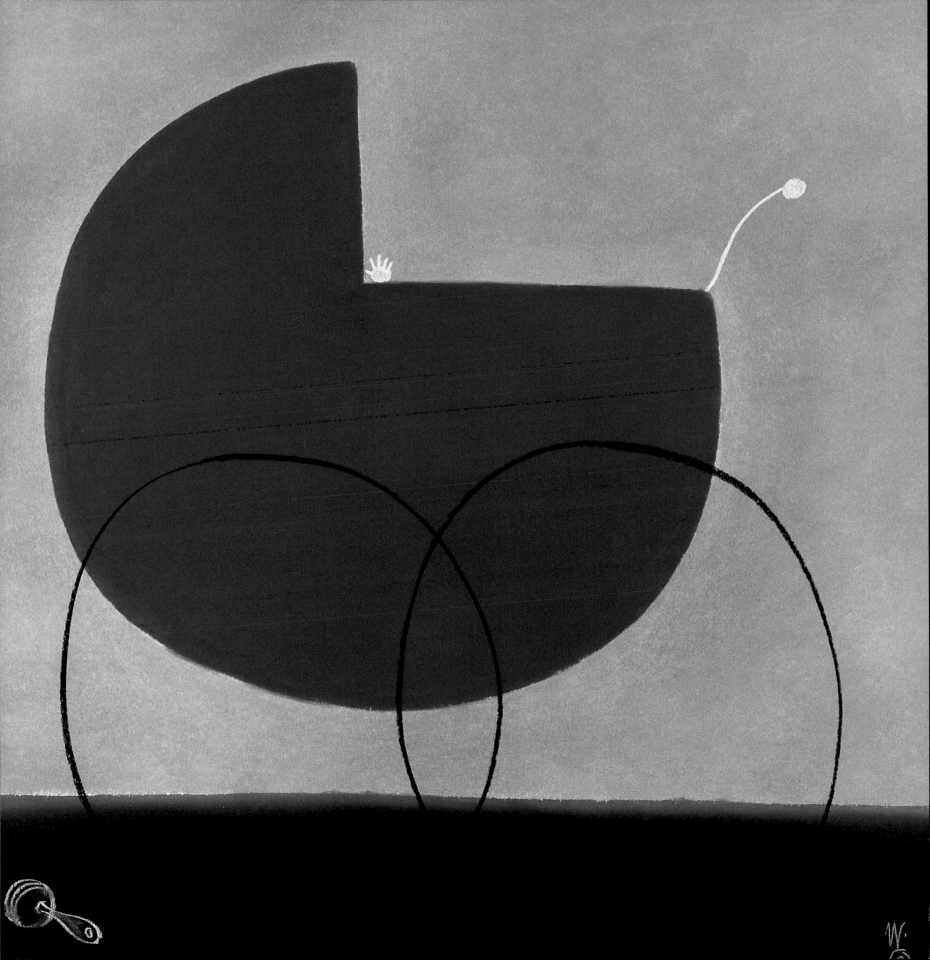

Previous page
Rattle and Hum

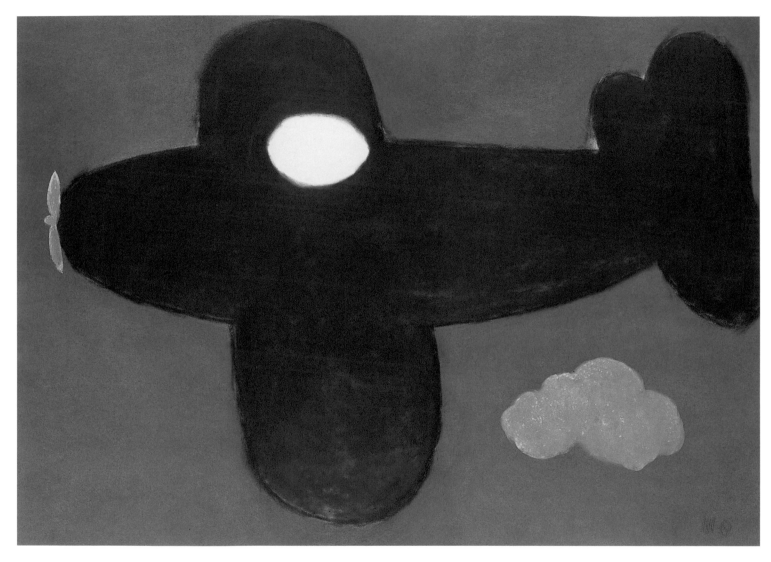

Flying Away

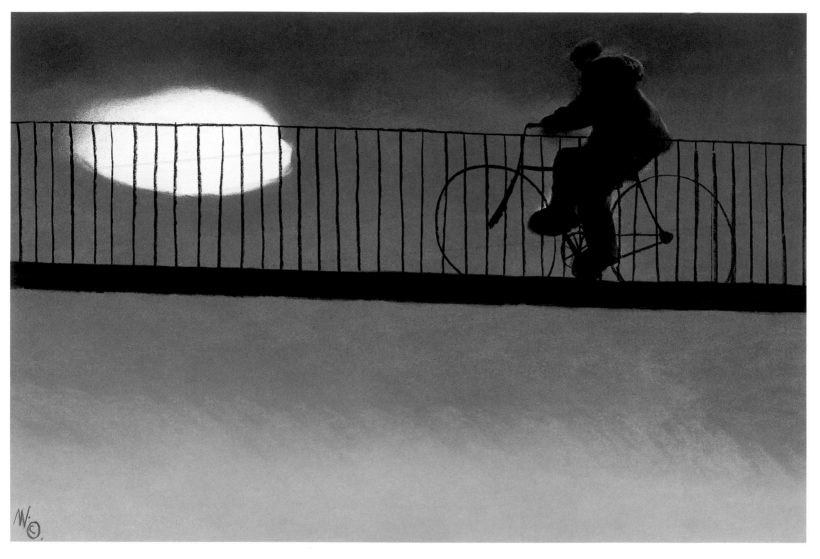

Chasing a Cloud

BRIDGES Certain symbols continue to reappear in my work. I work on and around them for a time and then move on, only to return to them on some later date.

In my earlier work you rarely see bridges—I just didn't draw them. Then suddenly they were there, in industrial scenes with chimney stacks and smoke. Maybe the bridge symbolizes finding ways around the obstacles, over the obstacles, getting into new environments, meeting new challenges. Or maybe just moving forward, going from one place to the next. I think that's part of what I'm doing in my life.

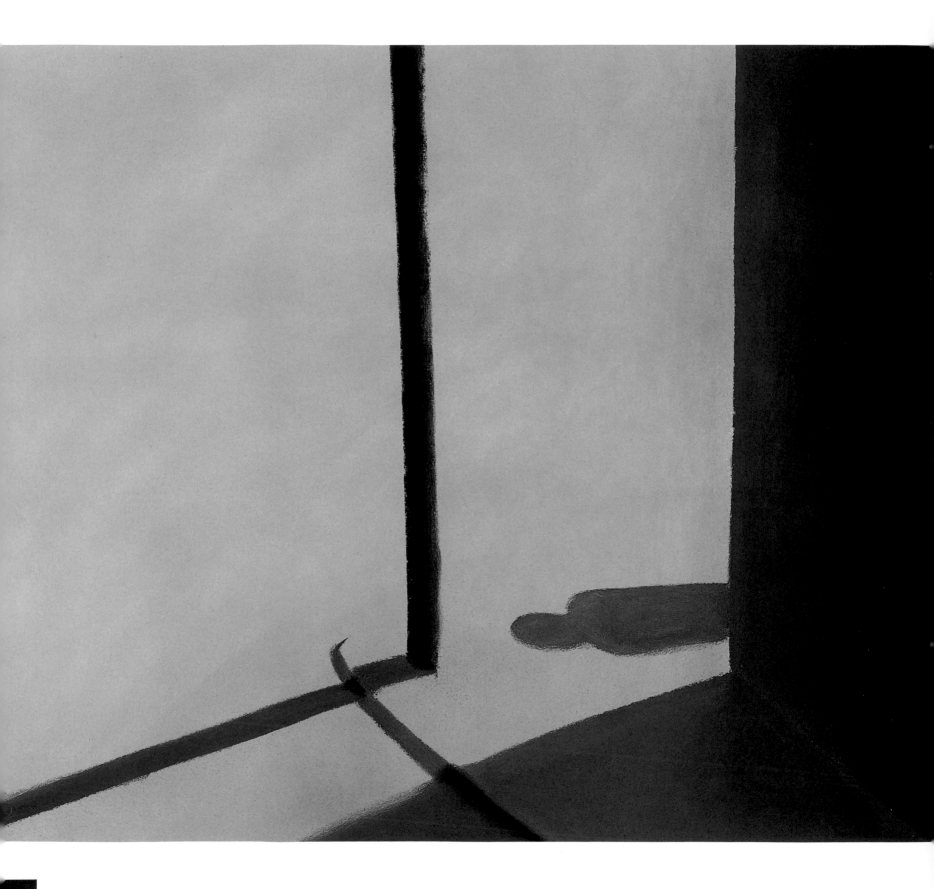

Man Walking

I can
Live
Forever
In your
Trust
Of hope

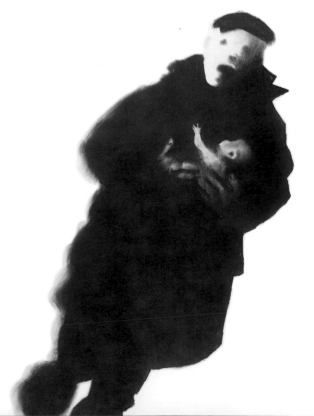

Holding on to Life

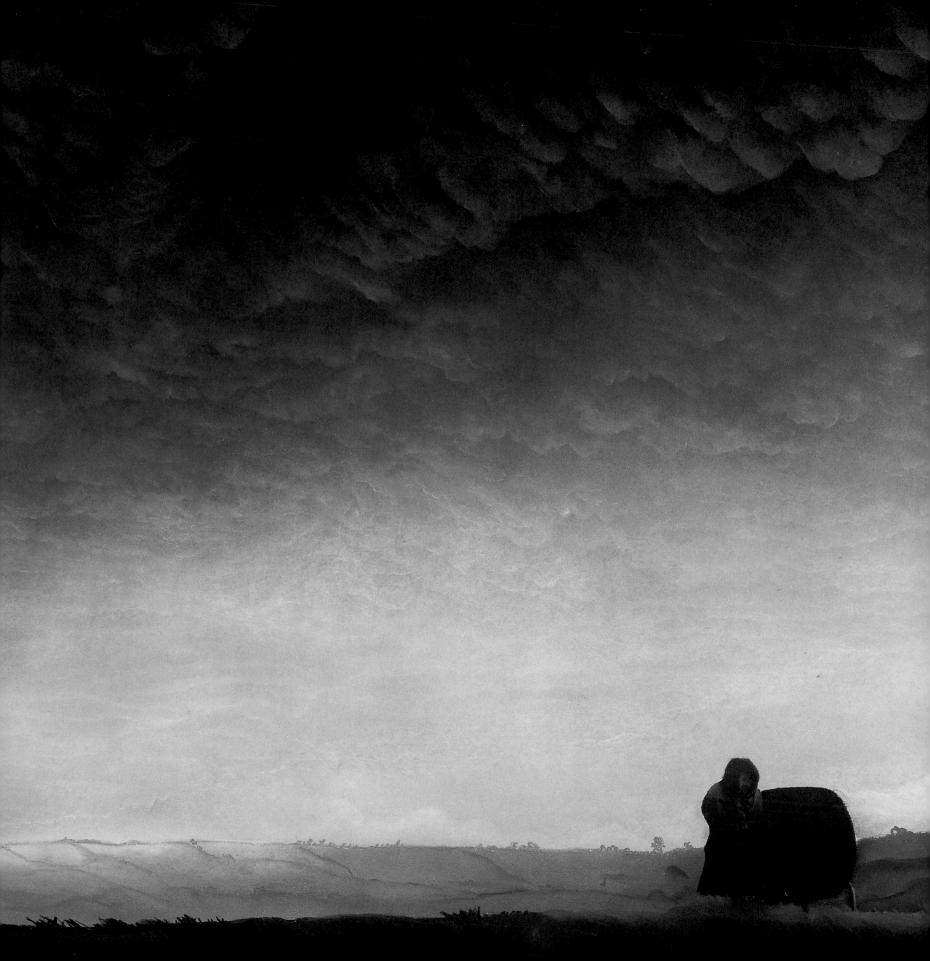

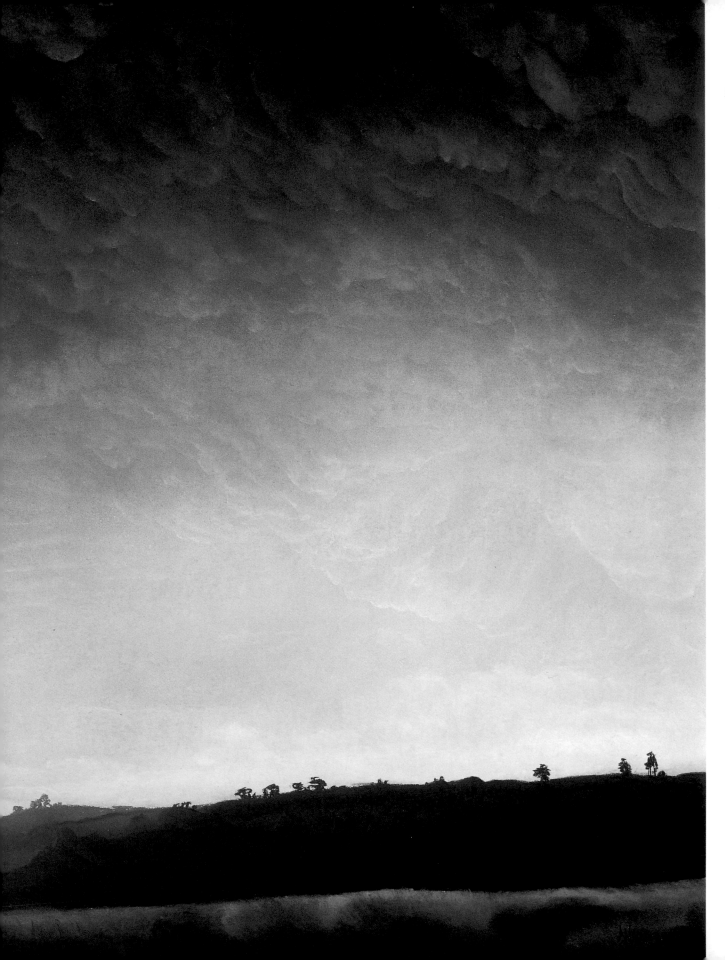

Soon Home

In this world
Of despair
There is an
Overwhelming   Man By Pain
Abundance
of Hope

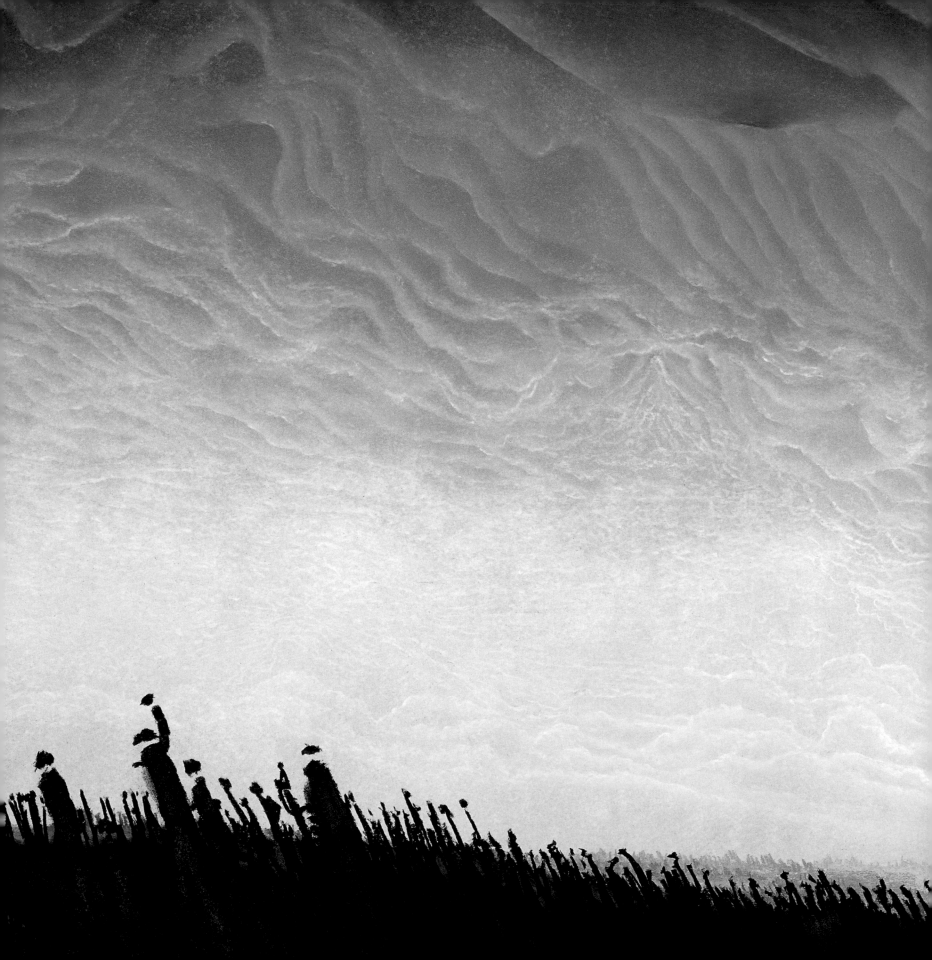

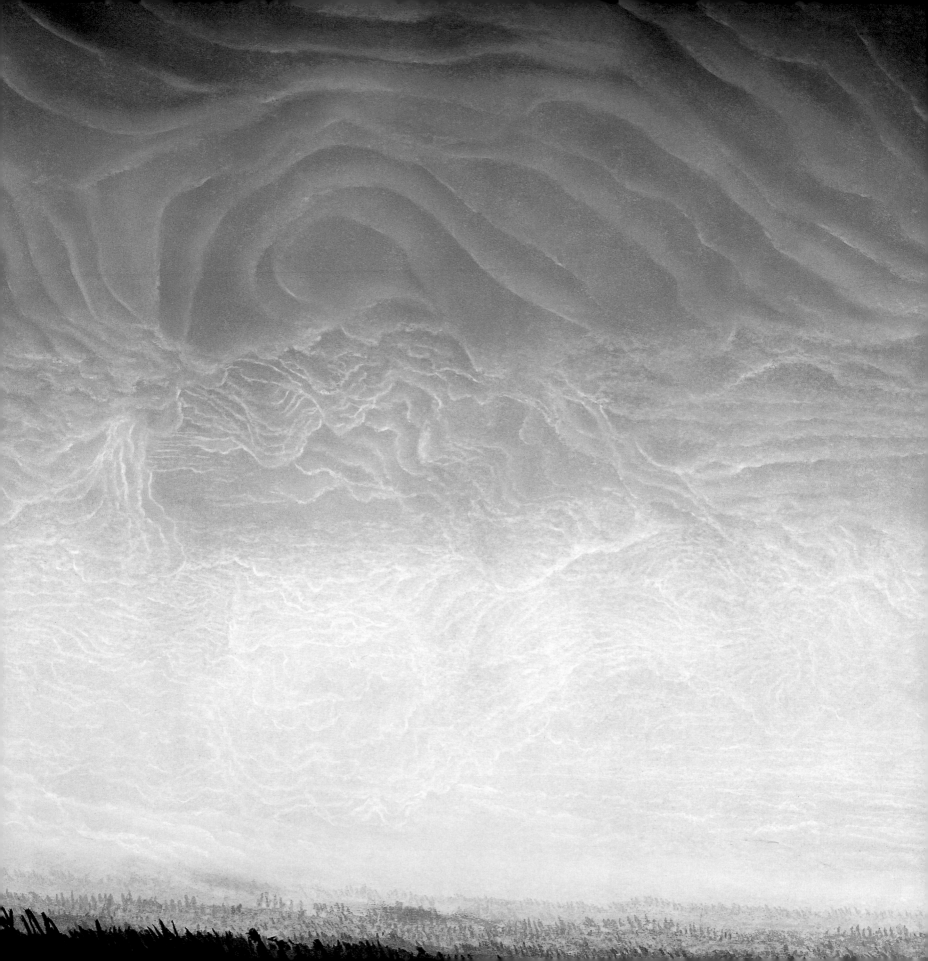

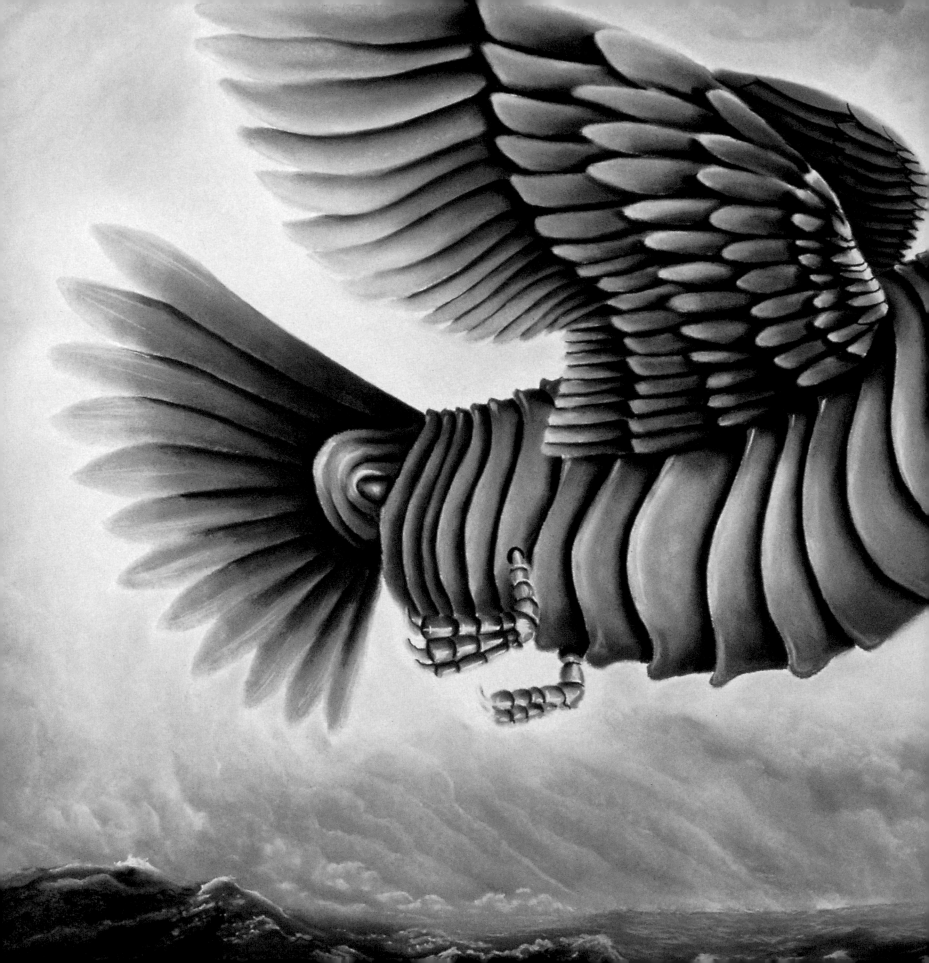

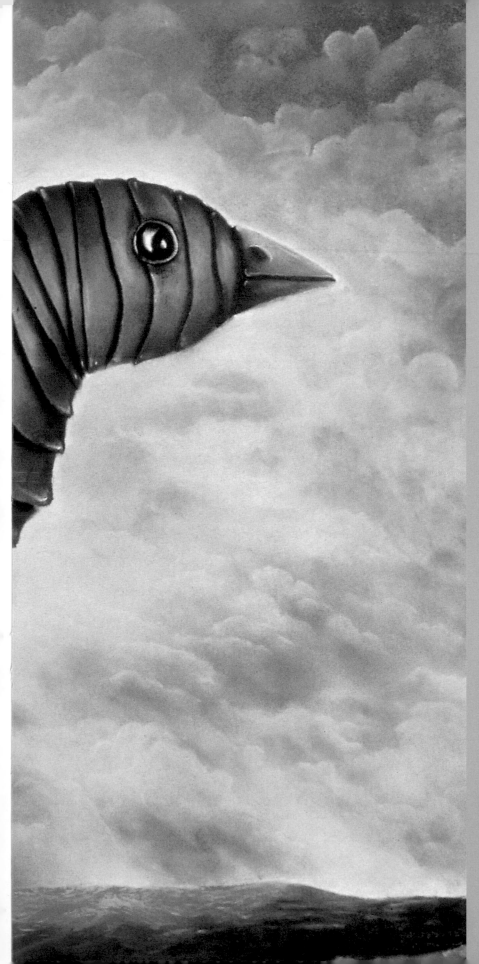

CLOUDS Every cloud is a struggle, every ripple a hardship. But at the same time there is always light breaking through. In life you need to experience both sides of this sky to gain appreciation for the light.

Crossing the Sea

Previous page
Leaving Gamora . . . to the Promised Land

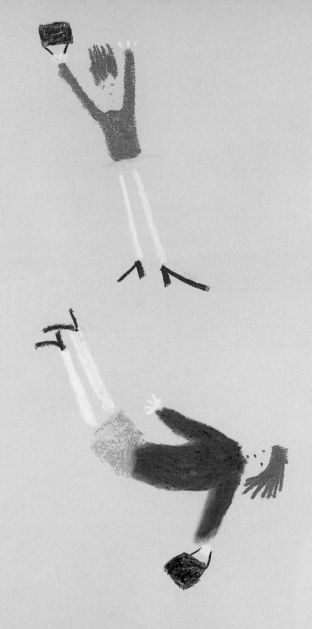

Index

Happy Landing

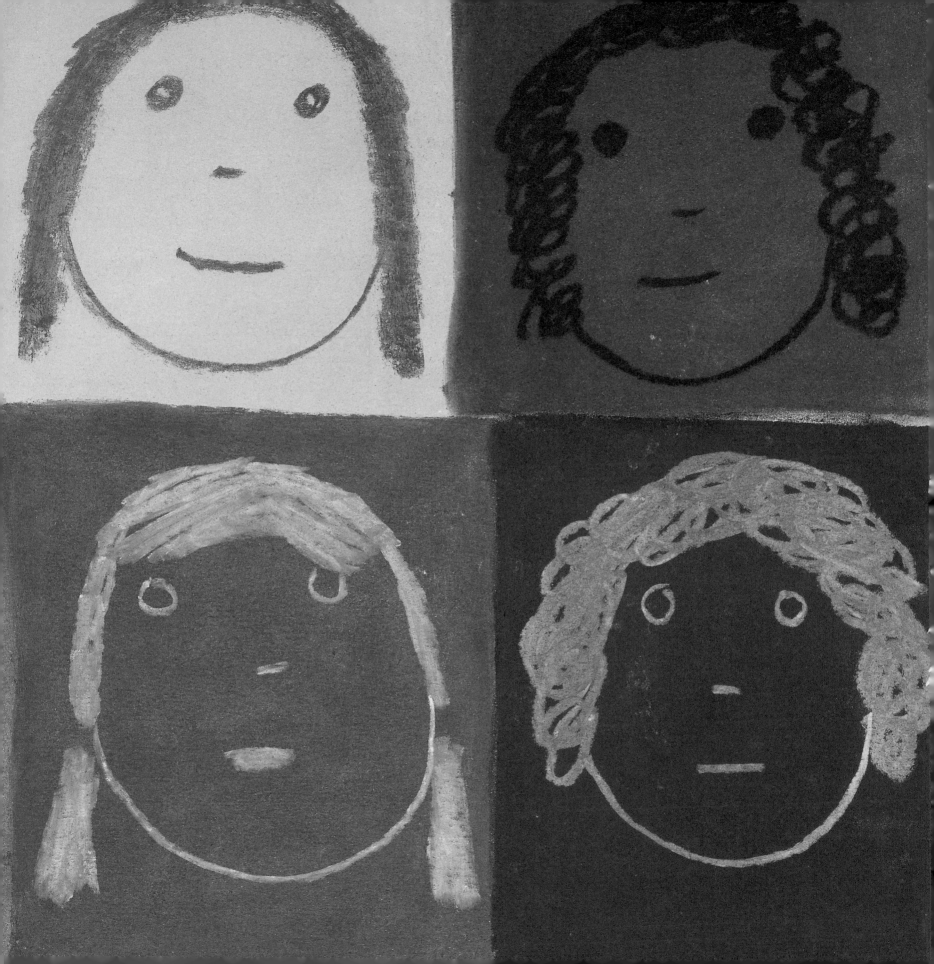